OTHER SMART POP YA TITLES

SHADOWHUNTERS
AND
DOWNWORLDERS

SHADOWHUNTERS AND DOWNWORLDERS

A MORTAL INSTRUMENTS READER

EDITED BY
CASSANDRA CLARE

An Imprint of BenBella Books, Inc.
Dallas, Texas

BenBella Books, Inc.
10300 N. Central Expressway, Suite 400 | Dallas, TX 75231
www.benbellabooks.com | Send feedback to feedback@benbellabooks.com

Printed in the United States of America | 10 9 8 7 6 5 4 3 2 1

Library of Congress Cataloging-in-Publication Data is available for this title.
978-1-937856-22-9

Copyediting by Debra Manette Editorial Services
Proofreading by Michael Fedison and James Fraleigh
Cover illustration © 2012 by Cliff Nielsen
Rune design by Valerie Freire
Cover design by Sarah Dombrowsky
Text design and composition by Yara Abuata, Silver Feather Design
Printed by Bang Printing

Distributed by Perseus Distribution | www.perseusdistribution.com
To place orders through Perseus Distribution:
Tel: 800-343-4499 | Fax: 800-351-5073
E-mail: orderentry@perseusbooks.com

Significant discounts for bulk sales are available. Please contact Glenn
Yeffeth at glenn@benbellabooks.com or 214-750-3628.

CONTENTS

INTRODUCTION

CASSANDRA CLARE

There's a question that every writer both is intimately familiar with and dreads having to answer. *Where did you get the idea for your books?*

It's not because it's a bad question. It's a fair question to ask, and it's not as if we don't understand why we get asked it—of course people are curious about the genesis of an idea! But the truth is it's very rare that any book or series of books grows out of one single idea. Usually it grows the way a rolling stone gathers moss or the grit in an oyster adds layers until it's a pearl. It begins with the seed of an idea, an image or a concept, and then grows from there as the writer adds characters, ideas they love, bits and pieces of their fascinations and interests, until they've created a world.

I've told the story of "how I got the idea for *City of Bones*," the first of the Shadowhunter books, so many times I worry sometimes I've memorized the story and forgotten the experience. So when I sat down to write this, I tried as much as possible to throw myself back into the moment when the first inkling of anything that would eventually become the Shadowhunter world crossed my mind.

I had just moved from Los Angeles to New York, and I was in love with the city. With its history, with its energy, its day life and its night life. My first roommate was an artist, with a deep love of manga and anime. She introduced me to another artist friend of hers, Valerie, who worked at a tattoo parlor. One day Valerie took me to the tattoo parlor to show me her book of flash artwork: It was a series of different strong, dark patterns in black ink that she told me were based on ancient runes.

Runes are really nothing more than letters in ancient alphabets. The oldest piece of written Scandinavian law, the Codex Runicus, is written entirely in runes. They don't have magical powers, but there's something very magical about them. They look like the letters of an alphabet that exists just on the edge of our imagination: familiar enough to be letters, but unfamiliar enough to be mysterious.

I've also always felt that tattoos and other body markings were magical—maybe because I don't have any of my own! Throughout history, tattoos have been used to show status or beauty, to memorialize the dead, to mark outcasts, and—most useful for my purposes—to protect their bearers and lend them strength in battle. As I stood there looking at Valerie's designs for runic tattoos, I thought, *What if there was a race of people for whom tattoos worked in an immediate, magical way? And what if their tattoos were runes?*

That was the first time I thought about the beings that would eventually become Shadowhunters. Over the next months, characters came to me: There was a girl and a boy, separated by some terrible fate, and a best friend, and a hard-partying warlock; there were vampires and werewolves, and an evil zealot who wanted to purge the world. And there were angels, demons, and other mythological creatures.

There has always been much argument among academics as to how folklore differs from mythology. I've always gone with the generalization that folklore tends to be about human beings or magical creatures (faeries, ghosts, elves) who live alongside them, interact with them, and share their lives. Myths, on the other hand, tend to center around beings far removed from humanity, often gods: The story of Lucifer's fall from grace is a myth, as is the tale of Zeus receiving thunder from the Cyclopes. I grew up on the urban fantasy of the 1980s, which mixed folkloric creatures like vampires and faeries with the day-to-day urban life of ordinary humans. I've always been drawn to folklore, but am equally enamored of myths, and as the world of the Shadowhunters came to slow life, I knew that what I wanted to do was create a hybrid mythological/folkloric world where the presence of supernatural creatures was explained by the existence of angels and demons, Heaven and Hell. Therefore, the Shadowhunters (also called Nephilim, based on the biblical story of the Nephilim, "giants among men") had been created by an angel. Faeries were the offspring of demons and angels; warlocks the offspring of demons and humans. Our world's folkloric tales of vampires, werewolves, faeries, and witches still held true, in this world—it was just that only the Nephilim knew their true ancestry as creatures of angelic or demonic origin.

All that was a huge amount of fun to develop, but unfortunately it's all world, no story. Plot, as Aristotle famously said, is character determined by action; no people, no story. I set about to people my world: I knew I wanted the story to center on a tough, strong girl with a reckless streak and a big heart. So Clary was born. I wanted to give her a best friend who would always be there for her, since the romance of a great friendship has always fascinated me. Along came Simon. And I've always loved the fair-haired rogue with a biting sense of humor who used that humor as a defense mechanism—and then there was Jace. Brave Isabelle, thoughtful Alec, zealous and misguided Valentine, supportive Luke, wise and wild Magnus, all came along gradually, spinning relationships between themselves as they grew.

One of the great challenges when you're writing a book whose world is based in legends and is highly allusive to myths with a great deal of emotional weight—it's not for no reason that Valentine's last name, Morgenstern, means "morning star"; his fall from grace is meant to mirror Lucifer's—is keeping what is happening at ground level, with the characters, relatable. It was always my intention with Clary to tell the story of a classic hero's journey, in which the hero receives the call to adventure. (From the Wikipedia entry on the monomyth: "*The hero starts off in a mundane situation of normality from which some information is received that acts as a call to head off into the unknown.*" In fact, the non-magical humans in the Shadowhunter books are called mundanes, a term borrowed from my gamer friends, who call everyone who doesn't play *Dungeons and Dragons* a "mundane.") The hero confronts a father figure, dies and is reborn or otherwise transformed, and achieves their ultimate goal—unless the story is a tragic one. Clary's call to adventure takes place when she comes home to find a monster in her apartment and must fight it to survive.

The bones of the monomyth endure because the story resonates within some special part of our brain that is hardwired for legends. And there are endless ways to put flesh upon those bones; just as every human has a skeleton that looks similar, but an entirely different-looking exterior, the monomyth provides a framework for stories that, when completed, could not be more different. I had only two goals when I set out to write a monomyth story: that it not be terrible (fingers crossed!) and that it center around a female heroine, instead of a male hero.

The characteristics of heroes—recklessness, bravery, dedication to a cause, willingness to self-sacrifice, a certain heedlessness—are often characteristics we identify with boys. It was a great deal of fun to give them to a girl. Clary jumps first and asks questions later; Jace, who serves as a secondary hero, is often the one counseling caution. When Jace is the one counseling caution, you know you're in trouble; that, hopefully, is part of the fun.

And fun is what these books have been for me, for the past seven years, since *City of Bones* was published and as eight more Shadowhunter books have come out. An enormous amount of fun. Though I have invented new worlds since, the world of the Shadowhunters will always be dear to me because it was my first. It's been almost ten years since I stood in that tattoo shop in the East Village and thought about magical warriors; this collection of intelligent, articulate essays has brought me back to that moment and to the enjoyment of creating this world. I hope you enjoy reading them as much as I have.

When I moved to New York City, I realized I had to write about the place. Between the hustle and bustle, I saw the possibility of another world opening up, just beyond our vision. Once I could see it, the Shadowhunter world appeared everywhere I looked. Whether it was vampires loitering outside nightclubs or fey peering from the foliage in the park, the city grabbed my imagination and ran with it.

It's hard to say something clever about Kate Milford's love letter, addressed to New York City and to the uncanny ability of place to open up mysteries we never imagined we'd find. So I'll just say this: Right on, Kate.

UNHOMELY PLACES

There is the world you know, the world you have always known; and then you blink, and there is a place you never had any inkling of, and it spreads out across your eyescape. And then, most shockingly of all: There is the realization that these two places are one and the same. It turns out you never really knew the world around you at all. This is often the moment at which the adventure begins: Your street has gone feral and has carried your house and all of your neighbors' homes to another part of your city; your child is a changeling; your wardrobe is a doorway to a pine forest where it is always winter but never Christmas. Or you witness something that could not have happened: a murder, perhaps, in which three kids your own age kill a fourth, none of whom anyone but you can see.

Much fantasy and science fiction is built on the idea of stumbling through a portal of some sort and discovering oneself lost in a place that is wholly other. I confess that I have developed a preference for tales in which the already-existing world itself is revealed to be wholly other; in which, perhaps, the experience of *jamais vu*, or derealization, reveals a whole new reality. Some of this preference has to do with the kind of fantasy I write; some of it has to do with my love of places, of cities and towns and the oddities that make each place unique. Some of it—maybe most of it—has to do with my own belief that the world is much stranger than most of us are brought up to believe. History is stranger. Mathematics is stranger. Science is stranger—but you'd never know any of this if you didn't venture beyond the textbooks. Every place— small town, big city, you name it—is stranger. So I have a hard time passing up speculative fiction that begins with the premise that our own world is somehow not the place we've taken it for.

But the experience of suddenly finding that something familiar has become strange—or, possibly, has simply made known its strangeness for the first time—isn't limited to books. I recall that as a kid I was certain for a long time that my parents and basically everyone in my family had been replaced by look-alikes, a fear—in extreme circumstances, a psychological disorder—that's probably at least in part responsible for changeling lore and all those fairy tales in which loved ones are changed into animals or objects and can be brought back to their original shapes only if the hero or heroine can identify them. Heck, stare at a familiar word long enough, for instance, or write it over and over enough times and it will start to look strange too: misspelled, unfamiliar, even oddly devoid of meaning.

Really, though, "strange" isn't the right word for the effect I'm talking about. The sense of the familiar suddenly becoming unfamiliar in an eerie and uncomfortable fashion belongs more properly to the world of the *uncanny*.

The uncanny is such a bizarre realm of human psychology and experience that Freud wrote three very involved (and very strange, and arguably very conflicted) essays on the subject, collected together in a collection titled (appropriately) *The Uncanny*. It's been discussed at length by philosophers, psychologists, and theorists around the world. When you read about the uncanny, certain motifs repeat themselves, and certain experiences appear to be common triggers of this feeling of unease and unfamiliarity. Ernst Jentsch, one of the early writers on the subject, attributed the sense of the uncanny at least in part to an intellectual uncertainty—the idea that one can't know precisely what one is seeing or experiencing, or can't know whether one's interpretation of the thing or experience is correct. In "On the Psychology of the Uncanny" written in 1906, Jentsch argued that the discomfort associated with the uncanny stems from a desire for certainty about one's understanding of the world and that this desire itself stems from a human need to feel at home or at least capable of survival in a world that may otherwise seem essentially unknowable, even potentially hostile:

> The human desire for the intellectual mastery of one's environment is a strong one. Intellectual certainty provides psychical shelter in the struggle for existence. However it came to be, it signifies a defensive position against the assault of hostile forces, and the lack of such certainty is equivalent to lack of cover in the episodes of that never-ending war of the human and organic world for the sake of which the strongest and most impregnable bastions of science were erected.

Among the most potent of things that may evoke this perilous uncertainty, Jentsch asserts, "there is one in particular that is able to develop a fairly regular, powerful and very general effect: namely, doubt as to whether an apparently living being really is animate and, conversely, doubt as to whether a lifeless object may not in fact be animate." This, he says, is what lies behind the human horror of automata, cadavers, death's-heads, and the like.

In his 1918 essay on the subject, however, Freud tried hard to kick this idea—that intellectual uncertainty is behind the sense of the uncanny—around the block, arguing that the skin-crawling response generated by uncanny triggers can be explained through psychoanalysis and attributed to basic human neuroses (or, rather, what one might consider to be basic human neuroses if one were, for instance, Freud) like the infantile castration complex and fears and fantasies related to the womb. He opens the first section of the essay by announcing that both of his courses of investigation into the uncanny (semantic and impressionistic) "lead to the same conclusion—that the uncanny is that species of the frightening that goes back to what was once well known and had long been familiar." By the end of the third section, however, Freud rather meekly suggested that perhaps the sources of the intellectual and emotional responses elicited by the uncanny are not as easy to analyze as he'd hoped— or at least that the uncanny in fiction might be a different sort of beast altogether:

> The uncanny we find in fiction—in creative writing, imaginative literature—actually deserves to be considered separately. It is above all much richer than what we know from experience; it embraces the whole of this and something else besides, something that is wanting in real life. The distinction between what is repressed and what is surmounted cannot be transferred to the uncanny in literature without substantial modification, because the realm of the imagination depends for its validity on its contents being exempt from the reality test...Fiction affords possibilities for a sense of the uncanny that would not be available in real life.

(I think that he's wrong there, by the way. I think real life affords *plenty* of possibilities for a sense of the uncanny, even of the varieties that Freud claims are only available in fiction. I think that attempting to explain them all away with complexes and repression is a bit shortsighted. But then I am not a psychoanalyst. Grain of salt.)

For both Jentsch and Freud, the uncanny is thick with the presence of the occult—meaning the "hidden"—made visible, and an unclear division between the living and the dead, the animate and the inanimate. It is populated by things that should be hidden but are not, things that have been carefully hidden that have come to light, and things that exist in the hidden margins, briefly glimpsed. It's a realm of things that are not what they seem to be, of hidden desires and hidden knowledge and hidden pasts, of mistaken identities and darkness made visible, of madness and inner worlds projected outward, a world where the simple answer is highly suspect and the irrational and otherworldly answer, while perhaps never provable, can never be completely ruled out. It is a place of ultimate uncertainty. The bizarre things you feel might be just your imagination acting up, or your imagination might be the only thing that sees you safely through the perils you sense moving soundlessly around you in the dark of your room. The uncanny is a grim and ghostly entity, inching toward you in the shadows that cut across a bright afternoon when your skin prickles and there is no breeze to blame.

There are endless linguistic discussions about the etymology of the word "uncanny," its opposites, and the myriad ways of translating them. For my purposes, it's the German that's most relevant. In German, "uncanny" becomes *unheimlich*, which translates more literally to *un-homely*. Not like home.

Dorothy murmurs it like a prayer: *There's no place like home, there's no place like home.* But if home suddenly becomes not like home, what then?

~

I can't actually remember what made me pick up *City of Bones* for the first time. I do know it was long after I had begun to call New York City home, and I can tell you exactly where I became a fan of Clary Fray. That was on page sixty-eight, when, accused of being from New Jersey, she retorts indignantly, "I'm from Brooklyn!"

New York may have taken time to acclimate to, but Brooklyn I loved from the first minute. Brooklyn does that to you. It makes you possessive of it. It makes you love it. Clary's fierce declaration was only the first of many points when I thought to myself, *This book gets my city right.*

There are plenty of other little details in the books that are spot-on if you've lived here. There is the constant and interesting problem of getting from point A to point B. Subway? Cab? Walk? Borrow a car? Where will you park? Is time of the essence? That's a problem, because you can't get anywhere outside of a ten-block radius in less than half an hour, and anyone who says otherwise—such as, for instance, the real estate agent from whom my roommate and I rented our first apartment—is lying to you. You always tell the cabbie you're going to Brooklyn after you're already inside with the door shut because no cabbie *wants* to drive you to Brooklyn, where chances of catching a fare back into Manhattan are so slim. Also, just like the windowless, slump-roofed Taki's, the best restaurants in the city will always look like dives, as if they have glamours hiding them from tourists. And people really do think coffee ought to come by default with three sugars.

But the most meaningful true-to-New York thing of all is the way the city is such a compelling, uncanny beast and forces Clary to adapt. This is why, despite the titles, Clary Fray's story isn't about the hidden cities of bones, of ashes, of glass. Her story is about New York, and about a girl finding her place in it and learning to love and trust it again even though it has kept so much hidden from her. At least that's how it seems to me, someone who loves cities and towns and who, when she first moved to New York City, wanted so desperately to love it but had to learn its true character, find its hidden charms, and accept its all-too-visible flaws before she could walk comfortably through it, to say nothing of finding its hidden beauty and mystery.

Clary's New York is both the one she grew up in and the one she didn't know existed and yet can't unsee or deny. Mundane New York or Shadowhunter New York, it's always *her* New York, and not simply because, by birth, she has a key part to play in the intrigues of the Nephilim. It's her New York because Clary identifies strongly with it. It's where she grew up and where she lives. Even if escaping its newfound strangeness were as simple as moving away—and it isn't, nor is it generally that simple in real life—that isn't an option, because Clary loves her home and goes on loving it even as it reveals itself to be something different from what she had always assumed it to be. Places, like people, are complex, and loving them isn't simple.

Of course, it isn't just New York that she must adjust to as she begins to see through the glamours that have been hiding reality from her for her entire life. As the proverbial scales begin to fall from her eyes, she realizes she has been blind to certain details about her own mother, and not just the past Jocelyn Fray hid from her. Even her mother's skin bears the scars of her early life, a detail that Clary has never noticed due to the elaborate spells that kept her from seeing the stranger world around her.

Then again, I suppose I always assume people are hiding parts of themselves from each other. People do that. Perhaps, then, it isn't particularly odd that all the family drama in the books never seems as big a deal to me as the shifting nature of the city, the things it hides and the things it chooses to reveal.

~

When I moved to New York City in 2001, it was unhomely in every sense. My apartment was a good home to come back to, and I loved it and I loved my roommate and I loved the neighborhood we'd chosen, but the city itself was frustrating, strange, and unwelcoming. I'd grown up in a rural suburb of Annapolis and I'd gone to school in bucolic, mostly rural upstate New York, but the city just being different from what I was accustomed to didn't explain what I was feeling. I'd lived in London, I'd been lost in Venice, I'd traveled alone in France and Spain, and I was about as self-sufficient as anyone I knew. And yet. It was almost as if the city were trying to knock me down a few pegs, trying for some reason to break me. It made me cry more than I was comfortable with. It made me want to move home to Maryland.

I don't really remember when I started to want to fight back. I don't even remember whether that's really how I looked at it. The way I remember it was that I started looking for evidence that this city wasn't what it had first shown itself to be. I started looking for what it was hiding under the indifferent, hurried, even cruel face it seemed intent on putting on for me. I started grasping at moments that weren't misery. Slowly, slowly, I found them. And at some point along the way, New York City began to feel like home.

Then, some time after that, New York began to change for me once more. Having found its homely side at last, I let myself open my eyes again to the unhomely, this time looking for the other hidden face of the city, its quirks and oddities and bits of delightful weirdness. When I'd been sure the city was out to get me, these things would have been lumped in with the things that made New York seem unknowable and sinister. Now, though, I discover those things and am fascinated by them without feeling that they make the city not like home. It takes looking around you with a certain type of eye, though. You have to be willing to walk down an alley just because of the interesting ironwork on the fire escapes. It has to occur to you to look under an awning to see the decades-old sign beneath, a treasure hidden (almost) in plain view. You have to be willing to look up occasionally, a thing that, in New York, where so much is going on at eye level, sometimes takes conscious effort to remember to do.

You have to force yourself to give things more than a passing glance. You have to look at a thing long enough for it to really show itself to you—a skill Clary has to learn in order to see past the glamours masking things all around her. "Let your mind relax," Jace instructs when trying to help Clary see a rune on his hand. "Wait for it to come to you. Like waiting for something to rise to the surface of water." Staring at the stronghold masquerading as an abandoned hospital on Roosevelt Island, Clary tries "to stare around the lights, or through them, the way you could sometimes look past a thin topcoat of paint to see what was underneath" (*City of Bones*). Seeing past the glamour—past the superficial—takes effort, but it's a critical step Clary has to take in order to reconcile what she has been seeing with what's really there and to walk confidently through the city she thought was home as something more than an interloper. It's the only way she can learn to navigate the once-familiar streets without getting lost, and without being afraid.

Every city, every town, hides beneath a certain amount of glamour that—either intentionally or not—can misdirect the eye or hide something worth finding. Learning to see through those glamours is part of the process of calling any place home.

~

I don't know if everyone goes through this passage, in which his or her ability to function as a complete person is somehow tied to the process of becoming functional in an unfamiliar place. Moving to a new town or starting college can be like that, although I suspect that the necessity of learning to function socially outweighs or at least overshadows the necessity of learning to function on the campus or in the new town itself. In either setting, it's more likely to be the people than the specific place that make you feel acutely like the outsider you are. There is something inherently stranger in discovering that it isn't the people that are keeping you from feeling like you belong—it's the place itself. Perhaps this is why so many people simply can't fathom living in a city (or, conversely, can't fathom living outside of one).

I also don't know if the concept of being lost still means what it used to. My generation and the ones that follow have been trained, if not raised, to navigate by GPS, taking the shortest route from point A to point B. We have been trained to use turnpikes and highways; if we have lost our fears of being lost, it's because the idea has lost its meaning. Take away our ability to know where we are at any given point, and I suspect we would immediately find ourselves in strange territory, even if geographically we are very close to home.

There is a very easy way of demonstrating the truth of this in New York City. You just get on an unfamiliar train

and take it to another borough. Pick a stop you've never
been to, and get out. Voilà! A whole new world. What's
even stranger is when you get out at an unfamiliar stop, turn
a corner or two, and find yourself at an intersection or a
landmark you know well. Because I like to wander both on
foot and in a car just to see where I wind up, this happens
to me all the time, but never without a moment's feeling of
having somehow experienced something uncanny. It's this
experience I thought of when reading the chapter in *City
of Bones* in which, on returning to her apartment building
in Park Slope and falling through a five-dimensional door,
Clary lands not in some other country or other world but in
the front yard of her "uncle" Luke's home in Williamsburg,
just a couple miles to the north, and still in Brooklyn. Even
places you know well can take on a touch of the unknown
when you arrive there from a different direction.

~

Cities have the capability to at any moment shift out of
the familiar, even if you've lived in one all your life. Turn
a corner onto a street you've passed every day for the past
year but have never actually explored. Walk home during
a blackout. Climb a fire escape onto a roof. Walk across
a bridge. Cities are brimming with the potential to reveal the strange; and it might not be that you're suddenly
transported to unfamiliar territory but that you suddenly
discover that the city around you simply never was the familiar place you (mistakenly) took it for. If you're of the
right sort of mind, it's a short leap from the strangenesses
that are part of any massive group of people living in close
proximity to a strangeness that seems like something more,
something eerier.

In a city, for instance, you are never alone. No, really: *You are never alone.* Disembodied voices follow you everywhere: They come through the floorboards from the apartment above where your neighbor is singing eerily out of tune; they come, disembodied, through the speakers on the deserted subway platform at midnight. It's very often nearly impossible to know whether you're listening to a live person or a recording. The empty train car that you step onto might be empty, but there are at least two people manning the train. You might never see them, though, so how can you prove it? Come to think of it, you might never actually have seen that upstairs neighbor. You are never alone. You are surrounded by disembodied voices and whispers, many of them speaking in languages you can't identify with certainty. Familiar, but unknown.

The uncanny is often tied to fear of the Other with a capital O. In a city, with all of its enclaves and boundaries, both real and imagined, its hundreds of different languages and faiths and faces, it is impossible not to feel the presence of those who are not like you and impossible not to feel like an outsider.

If the uncanny is evoked by the revelation of the occult/ hidden, if it is, again quoting Freud, "often... produced when the distinction between reality and imagination is effaced"— then the city is as good a place for the uncanny to dwell as any remote and haunted manor house. There are more hidden spaces in a city, more hidden lives and hidden emptinesses, and more darkened windows where shadow people pass fleetingly in and out of sight. There are more moments where the actual meaning of what we see or hear or imagine is obscured, more chances to glimpse a thing without understanding what one is seeing in the momentary, jarring flash of sunlight the train passes through between 59th Street and Bay Ridge Avenue on the R line.

I could go on, but the net effect of all of these things is that cities will always feel uncanny, if you are inclined to be aware of the uncanny at all. In Clary's New York, this otherness, this sense of crossing into someone else's terrain, redraws the map of the city. Chinatown is no longer defined by its Chinese denizens but by the pack of werewolves that dwells in the old Second Precinct building. Spanish Harlem is where the vampires make their home in an abandoned hotel. Central Park is full of fey. Industrial Brooklyn, a mishmash of artist spaces, oddball storage buildings, and manufactories that to me always looks to be in a strange state of gorgeous arrested decay, is where the High Warlock (hundreds of years old and himself an intriguing mishmash of demon and human) lives and works.

It makes such good sense in the books because these are places that feel unfamiliar in reality to anyone who hasn't spent time getting to know them. It's a short leap from this occasionally unsettling unfamiliarity to the enticing possibility of the presence of something truly otherworldly, something fantastic, something darkly magical dwelling behind at least one of the thousands of windows or the thousands of faces you pass on any given day.

~

In Jentsch's and Freud's essays on the uncanny, the revelation of the *unheimlich* is usually characterized by unease and fear—normal, understandable reactions. But the beauty of fantasy is that it allows the protagonist to pass through fear to come to know this different reality and to find a place in it. It allows the protagonist to accept the true, occult (again in the hidden sense) character of the place, to reconcile the mundane and the uncanny elements into a whole, to let go of preconceptions and expectations and open him- or herself to experience the full reality of the place. It is perhaps particularly appropriate that, after several hundred pages of *jamais-vu* experiences, Clary is allowed to experience the opposite: Magnus Bane presents her with the Gray Book and instructs her to stare at one particular rune. "Look at it," he says, "until you feel something change in your mind." It takes long moments, but then abruptly the unfamiliar Mark on the page has meaning. Clary does not suddenly discover that she has known this Mark all along, but she is suddenly able to understand its significance.

In stories like these, where the setting is a character, a major part of the protagonist's evolution is the passage by which she, suddenly marooned right at home in a place that isn't what she thought it was, must learn to love (or at least accept) the city. Only then can she truly take part in shaping the narrative. And there's no going back either. In the scenario of the uncanny city, the protagonist isn't questing for the portal home; she's questing for a way to *be* at home. This is a powerful message to carry back to the real world; for those who have experienced the alienation that the sense of *unheimlich* (when related to place) describes for anything longer than a fleeting moment, there are only two options: Go elsewhere, or find a way to survive, to belong, and, hopefully, to thrive. There isn't a portal that can whisk you home if you're already there, so the challenge is to understand and to adapt and to find the homely even in that which is not like home.

The final scene of *City of Bones* is a lovely visualization of this: Clary is presented with a panoramic view of the city, alive with all the things she can now see and sense but still visible and recognizable as the same place in which she grew up:

> And there it was spread out before her like a carelessly opened jewelry box, this city more populous and more amazing than she had ever imagined: There was the emerald square of Central Park, where the faerie courts met on midsummer evenings; there were the lights of the clubs and bars downtown, where the vampires danced the nights away at Pandemonium; there were the alleys of Chinatown down which the werewolves slunk at night, their coats reflecting the city's lights. There walked warlocks in all their bat-winged, cat-eyed glory, and here, as they swung out over the river, she saw the darting flash of multicolored tails under the silvery skin of the water, the shimmer of long, pearl-strewn hair, and heard the high, rippling laughter of the mermaids.
>
> Jace turned to look over his shoulder, the wind whipping his hair into tangles. "What are you thinking?" he called back to her.
>
> "Just how different everything down there is now, you know, now that I can see."
>
> "Everything down there is exactly the same," he said, angling the cycle toward the East River. They were heading toward the Brooklyn Bridge again. "You're the one that's different."
>
> …Her stomach dropped out from under her as the silver river spun away and the spires of the bridge slid under her feet, but this time Clary kept her eyes open, so that she could see it all.

And for possibly the first time, the sight is truly beautiful.

Kate Milford *is the author of* The Boneshaker, The Broken Lands, *and* The Kairos Mechanism. *She has written for stage and screen and, thanks to a deep and abiding love for strange and uncanny places, is also an occasional travel columnist for the Nagspeake Board of Tourism and Culture. She can be found online at www.clockworkfoundry.com.*

I love Sarah's essay because it cuts to the heart of the nature of a true warrior: the ability to work with what you have, and the ability to adapt. I don't just mean what you have materially, but what you have inside you: your background, the skills you possess, your ability to think on your feet. While everything else in Clary's life is turned upside down when she discovers she's a Shadowhunter, Clary's weapon of choice remains unchanged: art.

Beyond runes, which have remained the same for centuries, there is no precedent for Shadowhunters using art as a weapon. Luckily, Clary's pretty good at setting her own precedents. This essay is a great articulation of how she goes about it.

THE ART OF WAR

NEVER UNDERESTIMATE THE GIRL WITH THE SKETCHBOOK

Everyone loves a kick-ass girl. (Well—maybe not her enemies, but you know what I mean.) Whether her strength and fighting prowess come from years of training, supernatural powers, or a combination of both, she's a force to be reckoned with—and admired. We envy her seemingly effortless domination of her enemies, her killer instinct, and how cool she is under pressure. She has the strength and endurance of an Olympic athlete and the knockout punch of an action hero. Who wouldn't want to be like that?

But most of us, unless we're lucky enough to be born into a clan of ninjas, will never be that kind of kick-ass. I know I'm not. I could hit someone with a baseball bat if I had to, but I'd probably just hurt myself if I borrowed Luke's *kindjal*.

When I was sixteen, I dreamed of being a kick-ass girl—but my reality was the complete opposite. I was totally inept at weapons, fighting, and anything sports related. I could barely walk in high heels, let alone deliver a roundhouse kick while wearing them. And unlike the amazingly fierce Isabelle Lightwood, I didn't spend my teen years learning the fine points of demon slaying.

No, like a lot of fantasy-loving kids, I spent my teen years reading and drawing on any piece of paper you put in front of me. I read comics full of women with superpowers and fantasy novels with sword-wielding heroines on the cover. I might have felt like I was a hero at heart, but I wasn't anything like the characters I read about. Psylocke and Storm would have laughed me right out of the Danger Room, and no self-respecting party of heroes would have let me join their quest.

Which is why I love Clary. Clary is every bookish, fantasy-loving girl who grows up wielding a pencil and a sketchbook instead of mutant powers or a sword. She's completely unprepared when she's thrust into the world of Shadowhunters, Downworlders, and demons. She doesn't know their rules, she's never heard of runes, and while she can use a knife as well as any panicked person backed into a corner, that's not much help against a demon horde.

But Clary is also determined, super stubborn, and courageous. Just *try* to tell her she can't do something. When she finds out that Simon (currently in the form of a helpless rat) has been taken to a hotel full of vampires, she doesn't hesitate; she decides to save him, and she would go alone if she had to. Because Clary never abandons her friends. Even when she doesn't know how she's going to help, she's willing to put herself at risk to try, because, in her mind, that's what friends do.

Clary isn't particularly fast or strong. She's not skilled with weaponry, and she doesn't have magic, fangs, or claws in her arsenal. But Clary's a hero at heart—and that means she'll find a way to be the hero she needs to be, to look beyond the skills she doesn't have and draw on the skills she *does* have to ultimately save the day.

Draw, by the way, is the key word here.

The Girl with the Sketchbook

> *"But you—you're dead weight, a* mundane*." [Alec] spit the word out as if it were an obscenity.*
>
> *"No," Clary said. "I'm not. I'm Nephilim—just like you."*
>
> *His lip curled up at the corner. "Maybe," he said. "But with no training, no nothing, you're still not much use, are you?"*
>
> *—City of Bones*

Clary lacks special training—and to some people (like our friend Alec here), that means she's useless. She's not a warrior, so she can't get the job done. And Alec isn't the only one who feels that way. There are plenty of people who think that if a heroine isn't physically dominating her opponent, she's not a fighter, and she's less heroic than a girl who's kick-ass or tough. But not every girl can be Isabelle Lightwood or Katniss Everdeen. I think the true measure of a hero is what a person does with what they have, how hard they're willing to fight, and how far they're willing to go to set things right.

When we first meet Clary, her extraordinarily mundane talents include art, being a great best friend, and vetoing Simon's crappy band names. (Sea Vegetable Conspiracy? No.) She's the kind of person who doesn't hesitate to help someone in trouble—like when she decides to come to a club kid's rescue when she spots two armed Shadowhunters following him into a storage room at Pandemonium—but I doubt she thinks of herself as a hero.

And yet, when her normal life is ripped away from her, and her reality expands to include demons, Shadowhunters, and Downworlders, she doesn't hide from it. There's no doubt that she would be safer if she stayed holed up in the Institute (well, providing she stayed far away from traitorous Hodge and I'll-claw-your-face-off Hugin). No one would fault her if she wanted to sit back and wait for the Clave to deal with Valentine and rescue her mother. Just the fact that demons *exist* is a lot to take in—no one expects Clary to bounce back from that revelation and fight. If anything, they expect her to be a liability.

Because, as a girl with Shadowhunter lineage but no training, what can she do that they can't do better?

But Clary is not a hole-up-and-hide kind of girl. She's passionate and loyal and brave, and the fact that she's not a warrior doesn't mean she's useless. It just means she has a different set of skills to bring to the table—skills most people probably wouldn't associate with winning a war. But you know what? Those are the skills Clary has to work with. So she does.

She might not have been raised to be a hero, but she's so determined, and has so much heart, that she finds a way to be a hero anyway, using a talent she's had all along:

Art.

The Artist's Way

Art is a kind of magic. Creativity is mysterious, even to artists, who might be able to name their inspiration but can't always explain how their influences and experiences came together to create this new *thing*—this painting, this story, this song. If you break art down to its base elements, there's nothing miraculous about the letters of the alphabet or a drop of paint. But an artist can put those elements together to create something powerful, something that moves us and withstands the test of time. A work that no one but that artist could have imagined, let alone created.

Clary has that magic in her. She grew up seeing strange things like pixies yet never remembering them, thanks to the block Magnus Bane put on her mind. Even before Clary realized she had the Sight and that there *is* more to the world than meets the average eye, she was searching for something beyond the reality she recognized and remembered—and she found that something more in art. As Simon says to Clary in *City of Bones*, "All you've ever needed is your pencils and your imaginary worlds."

It's hard to imagine Clary without Simon—he's her best friend, and she would go to the ends of the earth to save him. So if *Simon* feels that Clary would be fine on her own, with just her art and her imagination to keep her company, that's a testament to how essential art is to Clary's life.

Art is magic, and art is powerful. Art saves lives—I really believe that. It gives us courage and compassion we might not have on our own.

When Clary's mother, Jocelyn, is kidnapped by Valentine, Clary is in desperate need of some extra courage and strength. And in that crisis, she turns to art—the thing that most connects her and her artist mother—to guide her. Art is Clary's foundation; it steadies her while the rest of her world is changing. So much so that when she's living at the Institute and feeling overwhelmed, she hugs her sketchbook for comfort, because it's such a familiar part of her life.

Art also helps Clary to cope with the strange and magical things she encounters. When she becomes conscious of glamours, she thinks like an artist in order to see through them: "Clary let her mind relax. She imagined herself taking one of her mother's turpentine rags and dabbing at the view in front of her, cleaning away the glamour as if it were old paint" (*City of Bones*).

Clary even makes important discoveries while she's doodling. One night she sketches some runes next to a drawing of an angel-winged Jace, then feels feathers when she brushes her fingers across the paper. Seeing that she can use runes to make a drawing come to life, Clary wonders if she can use runes and art to put an object *into* a page of her sketchbook. She tests her theory by drawing a coffee mug, then placing the mug on top of her drawing and sketching some runes on the page. Once she sees that it works, she realizes that must be how her mother hid the Mortal

Cup from Valentine: by putting it into a painting. And that means Clary knows how to get it out.

Art is a part of Clary, just like her Shadowhunter lineage—but unlike her Shadowhunter side, art is something she understands. She uses it to makes sense of the world, to clear her mind and solve problems. And just as she can relax her mind and imagine turpentine clearing away a glamour, she can open her mind to inspiration when she or her friends are in trouble. She's used to images appearing in her head—and she's used to taking those visions and letting them flow from her pencil to the page.

So when she starts envisioning new runes, she picks up a stele and does what comes naturally.

"Where do you get your ideas?" is a question every artist is asked, and there is never just one answer. Ideas come in dreams or visions; they can come from conscious thought or seem to take shape on their own. The concept of the muse exists because there is no one way of explaining how and why artists are inspired to create—and why, other times, their creativity seems to desert them. When in *City of Glass* Simon asks Clary where her runes come from, she says:

> "I don't know... All the runes the Shadowhunters
> know come from the Gray Book. That's why they
> can only be put on Nephilim; that's what they're
> for. But there are other, older runes... So when I
> think of these runes, like the Fearless rune, I don't
> know if it's something I'm inventing, or something
> I'm *remembering*..."

Sometimes new runes come to Clary fully formed, in a sudden burst of inspiration. The first hint we get of her rune-creating ability happens like this. When she and Jace are trapped on the roof of the Dumont (aka Dumort) Hotel, seconds away from being caught by the werewolves and vampires that are chasing them, they need to find a way off the roof, and Clary envisions a rune shaped like wings. Jace commandeers one of the vampires' flying motorcycles before Clary has a chance to test that rune, but we—the readers—are pretty sure it was a Flight rune, and it's a tantalizing promise of things to come.

Some new runes take shape only as Clary draws them, as if instinct and need are guiding her hand—like when Jace is imprisoned in the Silent City, and Clary's so frantic to get him out that the simple Open rune she thinks she's writing knocks the door right off its hinges and unlocks every pair of manacles in the vicinity.

Other runes require Clary to focus on the essence of the rune she wants to create, as when she's desperate to follow Jace, Simon, and the Lightwoods to Idris, but the portal has closed and Magnus refuses to open another one. Clary grabs her stele, closes her eyes, and imagines "lines that spoke to her of doorways, of being carried on whirling air, of travel and faraway places" (*City of Glass*) until the Portal rune comes together in her mind, and she is able to draw it and open a portal to Idris herself.

Still other runes come to Clary in visions from the angel Ithuriel, such as the Alliance rune she uses to join Shadowhunters and Downworlders together in combat. I like to think the angel acts as her muse in those instances. Clary and Ithuriel are connected by blood, and that connection is part of what makes her runes so powerful, but it is Clary's artistic sensibility that allows her to take what she sees in those visions and make it real.

As impressive as Clary's new and amplified runes are, her power goes beyond the individual runes she creates. It's her ability as an artist to see possibility where others see a blank page and, by extension, to see victory where others see certain defeat that truly empowers her and allows her to challenge Valentine when the Clave is on the verge of giving up.

The Master Plan versus the Masterpiece

An artist is used to failure. Not every work she envisions is going to come out right the first time. There will be disappointment and torn-up sketches—but a dedicated artist knows to keep going until she gets it right. Sometimes it's a matter of rethinking the original concept. Sometimes the flaw is in the execution. But no matter *why* it's not working, an artist knows that the struggle isn't over until she chooses to abandon the piece. She has to be flexible and keep her mind open to inspiration—but she will succeed. Because she's learning, and getting better, every day.

Valentine, Clary's father and the villain whose search for the Mortal Instruments sets the Mortal War in motion, is not an artist. He's a Shadowhunter warrior who believes in physical strength above all else, a narrow-minded megalomaniac and a first-class manipulator who lets his "son" Jace take a bath in spaghetti on his birthday but also breaks the neck of Jace's pet falcon, just to teach Jace the lesson that "to love is to destroy" ... which I guess means that Valentine really, really loves the Clave, his family, and Downworlders, because he wants to destroy all of that and rebuild it to suit his "pure" sensibilities. This is the guy who, when his best friend, Lucian, got turned into a werewolf, offered him a knife and told him to do the right thing and kill himself. We can see how far the Clary apple falls from the Valentine tree just by how they treat their BFFs, both of whom became Downworlders, interestingly enough.

Like most villains, Valentine has a master plan. And because his enemies believed he was dead for over sixteen years, he's had more than enough time to perfect it. He has spies on his side; he's bolstered himself with demon and angel blood; he even has a part-demonic secret son to unleash. He can predict the Clave's every move and counter it. By the time he makes his play for the Mortal Cup, he's confident no one can stand in his way.

Valentine knows he has to gather the Mortal Instruments in order to gain the power to bring the Clave to its knees and make his dream of a "pure" world a reality: first the Mortal Cup, then the Mortal Sword, then the Mortal Mirror. When he has all three Mortal Instruments, he can summon the angel Raziel and compel him to cleanse the world of "corrupt" Shadowhunters and Downworlders ("corrupt" meaning anyone who's not on Valentine's side).

Valentine has planned for every contingency he can imagine, but he has a weakness: His imagination only stretches so far. He's two steps ahead of everyone...except Clary.

Clary's a dreamer. For years, she's faced the blank page and filled it with figures from her fantasies or careful depictions of things she's seen. As an artist, her imagination isn't fettered by the constraints of reality.

Valentine is playing by a specific set of rules—he expects to win because he has what he believes is a road map to victory. Clary, a creative thinker, is unpredictable—she doesn't play by Valentine's rules, she makes her own. And she uses her imagination—her ability to think outside the Gray Book—to stop Valentine at every turn.

When Jace asks Clary if she can create a Fearless rune, she focuses, goes into that artistic zone that even Simon can't pull her out of, and draws a rune no one has seen before. It's Clary's Fearless rune that enables Jace to withstand the Greater Demon Agramon's fear attack when Valentine unleashes him in *City of Ashes*. Valentine used Agramon to murder a Silent City's worth of Silent Brothers, but Jace can't be undone by his worst fear, thanks to the strength Clary has drawn onto his skin.

When Valentine's demon army is busy making short work of the Shadowhunters on board Valentine's Ship of Evil (note: not its actual name), Clary is the one who demolishes her father's plans by dismantling the entire ship with her superpowered Rune of Opening. Nuts, bolts, walls, floors, everything falls apart—as does Valentine's victory. Clary can't beat him in combat, so she ends the battle by destroying his battleground instead.

And when the Clave is about to surrender to Valentine's demands, because they're certain they can't win against "every demon the Mortal Sword can summon" (*City of Glass*), Clary is the one who insists that the fight isn't over yet. She brings the Shadowhunters and Downworlders together by creating a rune that even Downworlders can wear: an Alliance rune that allows pairs of Shadowhunters and Downworlders to fight together and to draw on each other's strengths. And, by insisting they team up—"if you don't fight beside them, the runes won't work" (*City of Glass*)— Clary is creating not just a temporary magical alliance but, potentially, a lasting one. She's helping to break down the

walls of misunderstanding and fear that have kept the Shadowhunters and Downworlders from being true allies.

The bonding of Shadowhunters and Downworlders is
a development that Valentine never could have foreseen—
because, aside from it being unlikely, prior to Clary's Alliance rune, it simply wasn't possible. And the Alliance rune
is an especially apt way to challenge Valentine, because he
has been bitterly jealous of the Downworlders' powers for
years. He went so far as to imprison Downworlder "speci-
mens" in an underground lab, where he experimented on
and tortured them in an attempt to learn their secrets. When
Valentine similarly imprisoned the angel Ithuriel, initially it
was to get answers to these questions: "Why should their
powers be greater than ours? Why can't we share in what
they have?" (*City of Glass*)

Valentine hated that Downworlders possessed powers Shadowhunters lacked, but it never occurred to him
to try to share the Downworlders' powers peacefully, in a
way that would benefit both groups. His selfishness and
cruelty blinded him to that possibility, whereas Clary's
open mind allowed her to accomplish what her father
never could.

In the end, when all seems lost—when Valentine stands
at the edge of Lake Lyn with the Mortal Cup and Mortal
Sword in hand; Jace lies dead on the ground; and Clary
is devastated and hindered by runes that prevent her from
speaking, separating her bound wrists, or walking—she
grips a stele in her bound hands and, with a few swipes,
draws over one of the runes Valentine has written to con-
tain and control the angel Raziel. It is the rune symbolizing
Valentine's name, and Clary uses the last of her strength to
write her own name over it.

That single small rune is all she can manage, but it is enough. It makes her the master of the circle Valentine has drawn, which allows *her* to compel Raziel—while also stripping that power from Valentine, who picked the wrong day to incite an angel's holy wrath.

Clary has fought by using her art and imagination every step of the way. It's as if this battle against Valentine is her masterpiece, and she's signing her name to all of it. Her signature: the final mark you put on a piece of art—because she's given it all she has, and it's done. This fight with Valentine—it's over.

With one final Mark, Clary signs her name to her father's defeat and puts an end to his reign of terror.

She Came, She Drew, She Conquered

It's fitting that during the final confrontation with Valentine in *City of Glass*, Clary is unable to speak. Valentine has silenced her with a rune, so her last words to him—when he's finally seen her for who she is, instead of the weak little girl he perceives her to be—are not spoken but drawn.

> Clary stretched out her hand, and with her finger she wrote in the sand at his feet. She didn't draw runes. She drew words: the words he had said to her the first time he'd seen what she could do, when she'd drawn the rune that had destroyed his ship.
> MENE MENE TEKEL UPHARSIN.

Valentine has known about Clary's rune-creating ability, but until defeat is staring him in the face, he still thinks of her as weak. He underestimates her time and time again—

because she was raised as a mundane, not a Shadowhunter. Because she's an artist, not a warrior. He refuses to give her the respect she deserves, despite the fact that she has thwarted him multiple times, because he can't acknowledge that the way she fights back is fighting.

But a fighter is not just someone who dispatches enemies with a blade or a bow. A fighter is someone who fights— with everything and anything she has at her disposal.

Clary is an artist, and before she draws her first rune, she has never used her art as a weapon. But once she is faced with a war that must be won—a war that endangers the people she loves—she becomes an artist who fights. She won't leave this war to be won by others. She can't do it alone—but the war can't be won without her either.

The seemingly mundane, pre-Shadowhunters Clary who took art classes at Tisch, and drew fantasy warriors in her sketchbook, and sighed over cartoon princes probably didn't think of herself as a hero. But I'd bet that in her day-dreams, when she was busy drawing heroes or disappearing into a fantasy world, she felt like she could be one. Like there was heroic potential in her, just waiting to be tapped.

How many of us read fantasy because we have that same feeling? We live vicariously through stories, because our own lives provide so few opportunities for high-stakes adventure and noble sacrifice. And most of the time, even as we wish we could be like our favorite heroes, we know that we're just too different. Jace has killed more demons than any other Shadowhunter his age. Isabelle handles her electrum whip with such finesse, it's as if the weapon is a part of her. Alec's skill with a bow and arrow allows him to make shot after shot, even in a high-stress battle situation.

Maia's werewolf nature means that she's faster and more ferocious than any human could hope to be.

Clary, though… Clary is like you, or me, or that kid in class who's always drawing instead of taking notes. We *know* this girl. And that's part of what makes Clary such an amazing heroine. Because she manages to do extraordinary things using talents she honed during a mostly ordinary life.

Clary is what I think a lot of us hope we could be, if we found ourselves in her situation: someone who becomes a hero out of necessity, who is not on an even playing field with the rest of the players—but who, out of sheer determination, finds a way to turn her natural talents into the tools of her survival.

Clary saves lives—her own, and those of her friends. She draws a better world into existence, and she never lets the word *impossible* stop her.

In Clary's hands, the stele is truly mightier than the sword.

Sarah Cross is the author of the modern fairy-tale novel Kill Me Softly, *the superhero novel* Dull Boy, *and the Wolverine comic "The Adamantium Diaries." She's inspired by all kinds of art and illustration and curates a fairy tale–art blog called Fairy Tale Mood (fairytalemood.tumblr.com). You can visit her online at www.sarahcross.com.*

Any warrior worth his salt isn't too keen on having the secrets of his weapons revealed, but I find this essay by Diana to be an illuminating analysis of what makes Jace the Jace we know, love, and occasionally want to strangle.

SHARPER THAN A SERAPH BLADE

The Shadowhunters of Cassandra Clare's Mortal Instruments series have a variety of weapons at their disposal, and most possess particular favorites. Isabelle Lightwood is fond of her golden electrum whip, Luke Garroway (when not wolfy) is very attached to the *kindjal* blade Valentine gave him to off himself with, and Clary Fray probably gets the most mileage out of her Angel-given gift of rune making—that is, when she can manage to hang on to her stele. (Honestly, she drops that thing more often than Stephanie Plum forgets her gun.)

But Jace ~~Wayland Morgenstern Herondale~~ Lightwood—who, thanks to his angel blood, is one of the most powerful of all Shadowhunters, and who has more names for seraph blades than can be found in your average baby-naming book—has one weapon that trumps them all.

Humor.

Seraph blades and daggers and steles are all well and good (and for Jace, they're very good indeed), but the weapon he turns to time and time again throughout the Mortal Instruments series is his wit. When things look particularly dire, that's when his jokes get particularly harsh. Late in *City of Fallen Angels*, Simon even points it out explicitly:

> This was Jace being brave, Simon thought, brave and snarky because he thought Lilith was going to kill him, and that was the way he wanted to go, unafraid and on his feet. Like a warrior. The way Shadowhunters did. His death song would always be this—jokes and snideness and pretend arrogance, and that look in his eyes that said, *I'm better than you*. Simon just hadn't realized it before.

Poor Simon. Given the many times the ~~mundie vampire~~ Daylighter has been the brunt of Jace's masculine swagger, it's little wonder it took him four books to realize the truth behind Jace's weapon of choice. Luckily, Jace knows exactly what his biting wit, mocking laugh, and arrogant amusement can accomplish, even from the very beginning of the series.

In *City of Bones*, when Clary and Jace first return to her apartment, they are confronted by a Forsaken minion of Valentine's—a big one, with an even bigger axe. When the formerly human creature attacks, narrowly missing Jace's head with his aforementioned axe, what does Jace do? Does he sigh in relief? Does he attack the dude from a distance? No; he *laughs*.

"The laugh seemed to enrage the creature," who then proceeds to *drop his weapon*—you know, as you do if you're a possessed evil minion who is being made fun of by a teenager—and raises his fists to the heavily armed Jace, who immediately dispatches him with a quick slice of his seraph blade.

You know, as you do if you're a badass Shadowhunting teenager who knows that laughing at your exceptionally large, exceptionally enraged opponent is the best way to get him to do something dumb.

And the fun for Jace is just starting. Later, in the battle in Dorothea's apartment, he taunts the Greater Demon Abbadon in a similar way. As the demon soberly intones about his particular prowess over other demons and hellish domain, Jace feigns disdain. "I'm not so sure about this wind and howling darkness business…smells more like landfill to me. You sure you're not from Staten Island?"

Jace apparently knows that one of the best ways to attack the bad guys is to wound their pride. Abbadon does not appreciate his precious Abyss being compared to an outer borough, and leaps at Jace, who stands at the ready (are you noticing a pattern here?) with a couple of seraph blades.

Time and again, Jace returns to his signature move: Make fun of the villains, keep them off balance, provoke them into a blind rage during which he can coolly get the upper hand. He deploys his razor-sharp wit against angry demons, hapless rivals (Simon, when still vying for Clary's affections, was a common target), and even, on occasion, against Clary herself.

Even in Raphael's vampire lair, as Jace, Clary, and the beratted Simon are being set upon by a whole flock of bloodsuckers, Jace takes time out of his busy seraph-swinging schedule to ridicule Clary's Hollywood grasp of fighting (she thinks they should stand back to back) and mockingly call Raphael "inconsiderate" for daring to move while Jace was trying to stab him in the heart. His commitment to joking, even in a time of crisis, tends to infuriate his enemies. And, naturally, his list of opponents occasionally includes Clary, as his strong attraction to the little mundie deeply disturbs him (even before he finds out she might be his sister).

See, Jace never learned how to flirt properly, because he was raised by a murderous sociopath.

As it turns out, however, humans are a great deal smarter than Valentine taught Jace to give them credit for, and as the series progresses, he finds he can't as easily disarm and enrage the villains when they aren't simpleminded minions or demons (or, like Clary, deeply sensitive to his barbs). In Renwick's at the climax of *City of Bones*, his attempts to utilize humor against his father get him nowhere, since Valentine is way too smart to fall for Jace's tricks. Valentine is utterly without a sense of humor (so it must be nature, not nurture, that gives Jace his wit), and Luke and Jace's attempts to mock him are answered with dull, dead-serious regurgitations of Valentine's purity platform.

However, the attempt does provide the reader with a clue into Jace's internal state of mind. The more Jace distances himself from his father in that scene, the more his natural humor comes back to him. When Clary first finds him, he is under the sway of his father, and all of the teasing, all of the joking, all of the *Jace* has gone out of him. He's Jonathan Wayland: serious, earnest, in thrall to Valentine. But as he begins to doubt his father, the humor and sarcasm comes back, as much an offensive move (as useless as it is) as a defensive armor to protect him from the pain of realizing that his long-lost father is, well, not as great a guy as Jace had thought.

And the hits just keep on coming for Jace as the trilogy continues. Though he may have a way with wounding demons and minions through a few well-placed verbal barbs, when it comes to those with a little more brainpower and battle training—people like adoptive mothers, Clave Inquisitors, and his erstwhile papa—his attempts at using humor as an offensive technique don't have the same panache. Throughout most of *City of Ashes*, Jace doesn't triumph due to his sharp tongue; he actually suffers.

"Usually he could get his way with Maryse by making her laugh," Jace thinks when his adoptive mother begins to interrogate him about Valentine. "He was one of the only people in the world who *could* make her laugh." And yet relying on jokes and sarcasm backfires this time, and his relationship with the only mother he's ever known teeters on the brink.

Later, he tries to match wits with the Queen of the Fair Folk, who is admittedly amused by his comparatively pathetic efforts (and, you know, by the fact that Jace is *way* hot, and faeries like that kind of thing), but she makes sure he knows precisely who is the spider and who is the fly in her world. Though Jace mocks her with his now-that-you've-had-your-fun glares of doom—as Clary sees them— the immortal Faerie Queen can give much, much better than she gets from some teenager, even if he is a Nephilim warrior. Jace escapes from that little encounter only after being forced to make out with his "sister" in front of *her* boyfriend, *his* family, and the entire faerie court.

And he fares worst of all when he gets snarky with the Inquisitor, who calls his attempts at humor "revolting" and socks him in a magical cage, believing he's taunting her as one of Valentine's men.

The more subdued humor in this second installment of the series can be attributed to Jace's growing insecurity. He deploys his trademark wit mainly as a defensive move; he's trying to hide just how much Maryse hurts him when she doesn't trust him or just how scared he is of the Inquisitor's threats. He's no longer sure of his place in the world. In *City of Bones*, Jace is a Shadowhunter, the beloved (if orphaned) son of the late, great Michael Wayland (great in Jace's mind, at least; Clary thinks the guy's kind of a jerk), living happily among the close-knit Lightwood clan, dealing with his attraction to a cute redhead who, appearances aside, is *so* not really a mundie. By *City of Ashes*, the Clave is interrogating and imprisoning him, Maryse Lightwood has thrown him out of the house, people everywhere are calling him Jonathan Morgenstern, his dad's a psychopath, and—oh yeah, the cute redhead is his *sister*.

There are a few things that even sarcasm can't protect you from.

But when Clary carves the Fearless rune on him at the end of the novel, his sense of humor returns. Is fear of demons the most useful thing she excises from Jace at that moment? Maybe. But what if it's fear of everything else that's been messing with his head? With the Fearless rune on, he is able to kiss Clary, to joke with Luke, and to face a phalanx of demons with a swagger in his step. With the Fearless rune on, he mocks his father and acts like the Shadowhunter people have been telling him he isn't worthy to call himself for the entire book. Jace and the Shadowhunters, along with Luke and his werewolves, face impossible odds thanks to Valentine's mass demon summoning, but

Jace is back in prime form, yukking it up even as the ichor flies. At last, the complications of Clave politics and family drama and incestuous relationships are out of the way and he's back on familiar ground. Jace = badass Shadowhunter and demons = dead meat.

In the end, the fear demon Agramon manages to burn that rune off Jace's back. However, it does so not through physical superiority but rather by hinting at all the mental baggage the rune has been helping keep at bay. Agramon appears as Valentine himself, reminding Jace of their family connection, and even more, of how many characteristics they share: courage, leadership, and the arrogance that in Jace, at least, forms the core of his sarcastic armor.

And though Jace kills Agramon on Valentine's ship, the demon does a fair amount of damage to Jace first. Fear and insecurity have him in a humorless grip throughout most of *City of Glass*, as Jace begins to doubt not only his identity, but also his very humanity (or nephilimity, as it were). Clary notes his depression, thinking, *"Despair, anger, hate. These are demon qualities. He's acting the way he thinks he should act."* After all, like Valentine, demons don't seem to have much of a sense of humor. If Jace is Valentine's son, infused with the blood of demons (as Clary saw in the angel's visions), then a sense of humor isn't exactly his birthright.

Jace can pretend to be demon-tainted as much as he wants, can protect himself with anger and indifference instead of sarcasm and arrogance, but when the chips are down, he returns to form. When Jace is imprisoned by Sebastian later in *City of Glass*, bound, injured, and with no hope of rescue, he doesn't despair. He mocks his captor: "Waiting for a special occasion to kill me? Christmas is coming."

Sebastian replies: "You have a smart mouth. You didn't learn that from Valentine." You can say that again, demon boy. Sebastian, like his father (or perhaps his demon blood donors), didn't get a humor gene. He's also pretty smart, so he isn't particularly susceptible to Jace's attempts to anger him with his usual displays of mocking arrogance. "Nothing, not a flicker of emotion, passed across Sebastian's pale face," as Jace tries every trick in his arsenal, to no avail. Sebastian is weak, Sebastian is crazy, Sebastian is on the wrong side of history... nothing moves his "brother" until Jace stumbles on the deepest wound of all, the one that even *he* can't joke about, because he feels its bite so strongly himself. If Sebastian kills Jace unarmed and tied up, Valentine will be disappointed.

In the first few books, whenever Jace is given the chance to kill Valentine, he can't pull it off because he can't divorce himself from his long-indoctrinated need to impress the man he knew as Michael Wayland, the man he thought of as his father. His hand trembles in Renwick's in book one, and when he kills Agramon on the ship in book two, his first, terrible fear is that it really *was* Valentine all along. Valentine is Jace's enemy; he abused Jace, "beat Jace bloody for the first ten years of his life" (as Sebastian says in *City of Lost Souls*), but he's also the only father Jace ever knew. If there's one quality that Valentine has in spades, it's charisma. It's how he was able to get all the members of the Circle to do such awful things for him to begin with. Jace guesses right that Sebastian, despite his sociopathy and demon blood, worships Valentine in the same way everyone else did. And what's more, Jace understands that humor and sarcasm is not the way to convince Sebastian that he knows what he's talking about.

In the first book, Jace's momentary alliance with Valentine at Renwick's is humorless; in the second, his pretended defection when Valentine shows Jace his terrible plan is similarly earnest. Valentine's hold on Jace lives beyond his sense of humor, so deeply embedded in his psyche that he knows that the humorless, psychopathic Sebastian feels it too. So when Jace convinces Sebastian to fight him fair and square, the way Valentine would want (the argument is debatable, but hey, it works), there's no joking required, or even warranted. His connection to Valentine is one area of his life where jokes do not suffice.

In *City of Fallen Angels*, Jace is resurrected and reassured of his place in the world—or, at least, that's what he wants everyone to think. His cocky swagger and amused arrogance are on full display, but those close to him are no longer fooled. Clary, when confronted with Jace's continued vulnerability, thinks: "Alec and Isabelle knew, from living with him and loving him, that underneath the protective armor of humor and pretended arrogance, the ragged shards of memory and childhood still tore at him. But she was the only one he said the words out loud to."

No matter how hard he might be working to exorcise Valentine's twisted teachings, to Jace, emotions and connection are still a weakness, and humor is the way he tries to keep his distance from the things out there—demon or otherwise—that might hurt him.

An argument with Simon and his new roommate, the werewolf Kyle/Jordan, has Jace back in fighting form: "So basically you're threatening to turn me into something you can sprinkle on popcorn if I don't do what you say?" Exasperated, Kyle asks Simon if Jace "always talk[s] like this." The answer, to Simon's chagrin, is yes.

Later, as the demon Lilith's possession takes hold, Jace loses even this facade of sarcasm. Clary thinks "it was hard to see him like this, all his usual burning energy gone, like witchlight suffocating under a covering of ash." You can always tell when things are going poorly for Jace, when he's in the thrall of a master manipulator like Valentine or, more literally, when he's the pawn of enchantments like those cast by Lilith or Sebastian. When that happens, he's just not funny anymore.

In *City of Bones*, he has to lose faith in his father before he can join in on Luke's mocking appraisal of Valentine's plans. In *City of Fallen Angels*, it isn't until Clary breaks Lilith's hold on him by cutting apart his rune that Jace starts making jokes again, turning the full force of his humor weapon on Lilith herself: "You and your name-dropping," he mocks. "It's like *I'm with the Band* with biblical figures." ("This is Jace being brave," Simon thinks when he witnesses it.)

Lilith, however, is not amused. Seriously (pun intended), what is it with these demons? None of them has a sense of humor—that is, until Sebastian and Jace are bound. In *City of Lost Souls*, Sebastian and Jace go on a wild crime spree through Europe's most fashionable cities, living it up like a pair of hot yet evil frat boys on the spring break from Hell. Sebastian is no longer Valentine's humorless, sociopathic son. Whether it's their magical bond or just by way of spending time with a wit like Jace, Sebastian has somehow developed quite the knack for cracking jokes. The two of them even banter in front of Clary in order to put her at ease when she first shows up in their interdimensional penthouse apartment.

Clary is baffled by the Jace she meets. This time, his possession is of a different nature. He's not the despondent, heavily controlled automaton she cut into on Lilith's rooftop. In fact, it's hard for her to keep in mind that he's really possessed at all. Thanks to Lilith's enchantments, he is bound physically to Sebastian, his former enemy, and is also mentally subservient to Sebastian's will…but he's *happy* about it. He loves his new life as the sidekick of a psychopath, and, unlike the other time he was possessed, it's difficult to determine if he's faking it, because the central tenets of his character—arrogance, humor, and a passion for Clary Fray—are completely intact. "How could he be Jace and not-Jace all at once?" Clary wonders.

Every time Jace makes a sexy joke or brags about his physical prowess in that arrogant tone she's grown to love, Clary's confidence in her mission to rescue him from Sebastian is shaken. Maybe *this* is the Jace he was always meant to be: happy, funny, madly in love, pure in thought and purpose. After all, she's spent four books learning that Jace is *least* himself when he's not funny, that the jokes stop when Jace is under the thumb of a villain. But the Jace wandering about the streets of Europe and taking her to enchanted nightclubs is a real hoot.

Then, at last, comes that marvelous *Silver Chair*–esque moment, when the enchantment is temporarily broken and Jace urges Clary to believe that this, *this* is the real him and the other Jace is a mirage, no matter how "happy" (and jokey) he seems. But Clary remains uncertain. After all, she remembers the last time he was possessed, back in *Fallen Angels*. "You didn't smile or laugh or joke," she says, because she knows that's what Jace does. He smiles. He laughs. He jokes. And so does Enchanted Jace 2.0. But the Jace who comes to her with the *pugio* wound marring the red Possession rune on his chest, this supposedly sane, free-thinking Jace... well, he's deadly serious. What's a girl supposed to think?

Unfortunately, things get totally out of hand when deadly serious Jace starts talking about, well, *death*, and confused Clary decides the best person to help her out with the situation is her evil brother. Oops. Lesson learned, folks: Sometimes your hilarious boyfriend would rather be unhappy and unpossessed than otherwise. (In fact, when she goes to apologize to him at the end of the book, I initially figured it would be for squealing to Sebastian, not because she later, completely justifiably, stabbed him with a sword soaked in heavenly fire. Because, let's be honest here, which part of that deserves an apology? Obviously the part where Clary is a total tattletale.)

But while demonic bondings apparently can bestow a sense of humor on the likes of Jonathan "Sebastian" Morgenstern, we're all quite lucky that heavenly fire doesn't burn it out of the likes of Jace ~~Wayland Morgenstern Herondale~~ Lightwood. In fact, when Jace first wakes up, after all the burning and such, he almost immediately reverts to form, asking to see Clary ("'It really *is* you,' Isabelle said, her voice amused"), and, of course, cracking jokes about his dream life as a topless underwear model.

"God," says Clary, when he tries the same schtick on her, "I forgot how annoying the un-possessed you is."

Except she doesn't really mean it. Because in truth, she loved the sarcastic, arrogant, annoyingly funny Jace—loved him so much she almost let him stay bound to Sebastian rather than risk having him revert to the humorless drone she'd had the misfortune of dating when he was under Lilith's possession in *City of Fallen Angels*. The most insidious thing about the Sebastian-controlled Jace was how much like

Jace he remained. Enough like Jace that he was afraid Alec and Isabelle wouldn't believe he was cured when they came to visit him in the hospital. Enough like Jace that even Clary had her doubts about what was best for the man she loved.

Which means it's probably good for the Shadowhunters that Sebastian wanted to keep Enchanted!Jace as his own personal pet-slash-BFF. Had Jace not run off with Sebastian to make Mortal Cups and party with vampires, had he stayed in the care of the Lightwoods like some kind of rune-stricken sleeper agent, it's possible that Sebastian's terrible plan ultimately would have been effective. No one would suspect a happy-go-lucky, Clary-loving, joke-slinging, adorably arrogant Jace Lightwood of being a minion of evil.

Now there's a scary thought. After all, Jace did warn Clary that, under Sebastian's influence, he might "burn down the world…and laugh while he's doing it."

How very Jace, to make even the end of the world into a joke.

Diana Peterfreund is the author of eight books for adults and teens, including the Secret Society Girl series, the "killer unicorn" novels Rampant *and* Ascendant, *and* For Darkness Shows the Stars, *a post-apocalyptic reimagining of Jane Austen's* Persuasion. *She once spent a week in a haunted Irish castle with Cassie, so she knows exactly where Jace got his dangerous wit. You can find out more about Diana at www.dianapeterfreund.com.*

Ah, the Clave. Nothing like an intimidating, inflexible institution of adults who expect nothing less than unwavering, unquestioning loyalty to brighten your day. This authority is problematic in the extreme, yet so many Nephilim adhere to it! What gives?

One of the aspects I've tried to preserve in the series is the moral ambiguity of the Clave. They're supposedly the good guys, but they sure don't act like it. In many ways, the Clave begat the Circle, just by being who they were, as Robin points out below.

But ultimately, this essay is about growing up. It's about questioning authority, thinking critically, and coming into one's own ability (and willingness!) to make choices and take responsibility for them—an important stage of development for our Shadowhunter heroes and for us mere mundanes alike.

WHEN LAWS ARE MADE TO BE BROKEN

"We Shadowhunters live by a code, and that code isn't flexible."
—Jace Wayland, *City of Bones*

magine that your best friend came to you one day, brimming with excitement because she'd met these super-awesome new friends who suggested she come live with them, follow a bunch of arcane and unquestionable laws, and cut ties with all her old friends because they're incapable of understanding her new super-awesome life.

If you're a child of the '80s like me, reared on a steady diet of Jonestown horror stories and trashy novels about brainwashed teens, you would immediately recognize the situation for what it was: Your best friend has joined a cult.

If you're not a child of the '80s but not completely oblivious, you'd still clue in pretty quick: definitely a cult.

Simon Lewis is far from oblivious.

As he tells his best friend, Clary Fray, in *City of Ashes*, "The Shadowhunter thing—they're like a cult." Clary denies it, of course, because who wants to admit they've been suckered into a cult? But Simon's got evidence: "Sure they are. Shadowhunting is their whole lives. And they look down on everyone else … They're not friends with ordinary people, they don't go to the same places, they don't know the same jokes, they think they're above us." Simon may have a somewhat bizarre definition of cults—he could be describing a particularly snobbish bunch of cheerleaders—but you've got to admit he has a point. Like any good cultists, Shadowhunters forswear allegiance to anything that could interfere with their loyalty to the institution. (Remember Alec explaining in *City of Bones* why he wishes Clary would disappear: "[She's] making Jace act like—like he isn't one of us. Making him break his oath to the Clave, making him break the Law.") They share an eccentric but ironclad belief system and hew to a code of behavior that allows for no deviation. And let's not forget their utter ignorance of basic pop culture that could only result from spending a life in cultural isolation, willfully ignoring the outside world.

Admittedly, these days the word "cult" has a mushy definition and is easily pinned on any group with a suitably wacky set of vaguely religious-seeming habits and beliefs. But the Shadowhunters' odd fashion sense and demonology studies (a belief that doesn't seem so wacky once demons start popping up everywhere to eat people alive) isn't what raises Simon's hackles. It is (or should be) the isolationist and absolutist nature of the Shadowhunters that strikes Simon as threateningly cult-like. He's using the term as a loose stand-in for any group that dictates every major element of its members' lives, that conflates obedience with morality, that replaces independent decision making with knee-jerk obeisance to a "higher" law, running itself like a miniature absolutist state. Call them a cult, call them a mini-dictatorship, call them a really, *really* intense fraternity, but there's no question that the Shadowhunters are extremists, distrustful of outsiders, obsessed with obedience, and worshipful of the laws that govern every aspect of their behavior.

And the supposedly rebellious Clary—along with her fellow teen Shadowhunters—welcomes this life and its mandates with open arms. (Yes, she seems to have little choice in the matter, given the whole life-in-danger, chased-by-demons, need-to-save-the-world situations she keeps ending up in, but as will be discussed later, there's always a choice. She chooses to join up.) Not that the implications occur to her, or any of the other young Shadowhunters. In fact, Clary's repulsed by the thought of anyone voluntarily signing up for that kind of draconian existence—at least in the abstract. Upon hearing the loyalty oath of Valentine's Circle: "I hereby render unconditional obedience to the Circle and its principles"

(*City of Bones*), she's totally freaked out. "It sounds creepy," she complains. "Like a fascist organization or something." Somehow Clary fails to connect the dots to the Clave and the obedience *it* demands, an obedience no less unconditional than that required by Valentine. After all: The Law is hard, but it *is* the Law.

Questioning the Law is not only forbidden: It's considered a threat. Which is a strange situation for teenagers— for whom you'd expect questioning authority to be a prime directive—to find themselves in, much less willingly accept. And indeed, things don't go well for those who can't toe the line: It's easy to imagine Valentine as that querulous child who asked the questions no one was supposed to ask. *Why not just make more Shadowhunters?* he asked his teachers innocently—an idea seen as "sacrilege."

Why do we do what we do? Because it is the Law.

You might as well say: Because we said so.

Maybe it's not so surprising that Valentine stopped asking questions of his elders and started asking them of his peers—then, quickly, started supplying the answers himself. Nor is it surprising that he substituted one extreme for another. Young Shadowhunters may be great with a stele and deadly with a blade, but they don't get a lot of lessons in moderation and moral flexibility.

When it comes to rebellion, Valentine is the exception: For Shadowhunters, obedience (whether to the Clave or, for that brief period of rebellion, to the Circle) is the rule. Why would generations of teens, given more power and responsibility (not to mention more weapons) than any of their mundane peers, go along so readily with the dictates handed down by their elders? Why would the outspoken, stubborn, courageous young Shadowhunters of the Mortal Instruments series—and the readers who'd happily switch places with them—so unquestioningly buy into the Clave's brand of absolute authority and the omnipotence of its Law?

Speaking as a former teenager, I'd like to believe there's more to it than a hormonal attraction to fascism.

Don't Trust the Man (Trust the Institution)

> *"Betrayal is never pretty, but to betray a child—that's a double betrayal, don't you think?"*
> —Valentine Morgenstern, *City of Bones*

One of the great tragedies of growing up is the discovery that your parents—and your teachers, and your sports heroes, and your favorite actors, singers, YouTube sensations—are fallible. Adults don't know all, and what they do know, they often won't tell you—because they've got their own agendas, or because they want to shield you from the hard truths "for your own good." Adults lie, they betray, they screw up in every way possible, and the adult Shadowhunters are no different from their mundane counterparts—except that a Shadowhunter's lies are more likely to get you eaten by a demon.

The Mortal Instruments books are rife with adults lying to their impressionable charges, often in ways that nearly destroy the teens' lives. In some cases, this is simply because the liars are evil: Valentine lies to Jace about everything because that's what bad guys do. The more lies, the better to enact his evil plan. Hodge lies because that's also what cowards do, and when you're in sway to the big bad guy, you do whatever he tells you, especially if what he tells you to do is pretend you're not such a coward. It's more unsettling—and far more destabilizing—when the people lying are the ones who are supposed to tell the truth: the good guys, the ones you're supposed to trust with your faith and your life. The ones who tell you what to do and expect you to nod and go along. They claim they tell lies only to protect you, withhold information only "for your own good."

But it's not for Clary's own good that her mother lied to her for her entire life, stole her memories, allowed her to be taken unaware by a demonic ambush, and, certainly not least, let her believe she'd fallen in love with her own brother. As it's not for Jace's own good that Maryse allows him to believe she's exiled him from his family, when in fact she just wants to get him away from the Inquisitor. Luke lies to Clary about who he really is—and who *she* really is; the Lightwoods lie to their children about what they once were. Over and over again, these supposedly trustworthy adults abuse the faith of their children—and that isn't to mention all the times that adults in the highest positions of authority in the Clave abuse their power for their own misguided purposes. The first Inquisitor following her own agenda with Jace, the next Inquisitor following *his* twisted agenda with Simon, the shunning of Luke, the casual prejudice against and occasional abuse of Downworlders…it's no wonder that Clary, Jace, Isabelle, and Alec spend a fair amount of time defying orders. And maybe it's no wonder that, robbed of the ability to trust in individual authorities, they put so much faith in the authority of an institution. Everyone has to believe in something, and the Clave offers a ready solution to anyone disappointed by human fallibility.

People may make mistakes, *people* may lie to you and fail you, but the Law is incorruptible.

Clary and the others think nothing of defying their parents and only a little more than nothing about defying the Clave administrators, the fallible humans in charge. But it never occurs to any of them to defy the Law itself, to question, say, the rules about *parabatai* relations, about minors having no vote in Clave operations, about revealing things to mundanes, about reporting people to the authorities. They may question the adults who bend and break those rules, but they never question the assumption that the rules exist for a good reason. And, as usual, it's Valentine who goes the extra mile, who makes the uncomfortable claim that it's possible to question a law while remaining loyal to the institution it governs. (Uncomfortable, because who wants to agree with Valentine?) He refuses to let anyone call him a traitor, because "[a] man doesn't have to agree with his government to be a patriot" (*City of Ashes*).

Why are our bold, curious, stubborn heroes so slow to catch onto this concept and so reluctant to start asking the hard questions and making their own rules?

Maybe because when the rules of life, and the punishment for violating them, aren't spelled out in detail, figuring them out can be torture. This is especially true of adolescence, when your social fortunes can be decided by the most trivial of wrong choices: wearing the wrong outfit, saying the wrong thing, kissing the wrong guy. Most high schools are as inflexible and judgmental as any fundamentalist society—ostracism and exile for the most minor of infractions is the norm. Following these unspoken rules is hard enough…but what about when you can't even figure out what they are?

Clary spends much of *City of Ashes* playing at this, trying to figure out how she's "supposed" to act—as a girlfriend to Simon, as a sister to Jace—as if life were a role-playing game in which you have to work out the rules as you go along. (A game that poor Clary's pretty much guaranteed to lose, given how ungirlfriendy she feels to one and how very unsisterly she feels to the other.) It's only when it comes to playing her role as a Shadowhunter that she doesn't have to guess at what she's *supposed* to do, because people are only too willing to tell her. If you're forced to play the game of life, who wouldn't want a cheat sheet?

Power to the Powerless

> *"What?" Jace sounded furious. "Why not? The Clave requires you—"*
>
> *Magnus looked at him coldly. "I don't like being told what to do, little Shadowhunter."*
>
> *—City of Bones*

Just one problem: You're not *forced* to play the game. You can ignore the rules; you can make up your own. Magnus Bane is a living example, the closest thing the Mortal Instruments has to an anarchist, and certainly he's in no mood to be told what to do. His resistance to obey is no surprise here. The surprise is that a seventeen-year-old with no magical powers would think he could issue commands to the most powerful warlock on the eastern seaboard. But Jace can and does, without a second thought, because he's not just speaking for himself: He's speaking for the Clave, with the full power of the Law.

The trilogy is packed with the (relatively) powerless us- ing rules and laws to control the powerful—warlocks con- trolling demons and magical forces, Valentine controlling his demon army with the Mortal Cup, controlling Clary herself with binding runes—in all these cases, power imbal- ances don't matter. No matter who's stronger, the one with the rules on his side wins. And the Shadowhunters in par- ticular seem to conflate the laws of magic with laws *about* magic (i.e., the Law), assuming that both are immutable.

This is a big reason why even a self-proclaimed rebel like Jace might be perfectly happy there are so many rules: He's figured out how to use them to his benefit. The Law can be a more powerful weapon than a sword. No matter how young you are, no matter how relatively weak you might be, if you have the power of the Law on your side, you can push anyone around.

Well, almost anyone.

The problem with the Shadowhunter Law is that it's *not* a law of physics. It's a social contract, and as with all social contracts, its only magic is the magic of mutual agreement. Its power derives from belief in the impossibility of defying it—which means there's nothing more threatening than an outsider who can see the Law for what it is.

A choice.

Think about it in the high school context: A group of people—let's call them the popular crowd—ostensibly have no more power than anyone else. They have to go to the same classes, do the same homework, serve the same detention when they step out of line. But by mutual, unspoken agree- ment among the entire student body, this group has accrued a specific kind of power: the power to admit or reject other stu- dents from its ranks. But popularity gives you power only over people who care about being popular. Ostracism gives you power only over those who fear being ostracized. A queen bee mean girl can decimate her prey by insulting their outfit, refusing to sit with them at lunch, denying them an invitation to the most exclusive of parties...but what does that matter to the freethinker who could care less about fashion critiques, prefers lunch in the library, and would rather gouge out her eyes than party with the populars? And what would it do to the queen bees of the high school world if the student body, as one, decided that "cool" was worthless, and royal favor even more so? This is why the outsider, the rebel who rejects the social hierarchy—who doesn't care what anyone in so-called power thinks of her—is so threatening to the powers that be. It's true for the cheerleaders and it's true for the Clave.

The very existence of someone who defies the Law renders defiance a possible option. Something that Jace is the first to understand, when, in *City of Glass*, he realizes that the Clave will read Clary's rune-creating ability as a portent of doom. After all, the only thing more dangerous than a willingness to ignore the Law is an ability to change it.

Rebels Without a Law

> *"I should have warned her about your habit of never doing what you're told."*
> —Jace Wayland to Clary Fray, *City of Bones*

But rebels do exist—in mundane high schools and Shadowhunter Institutes alike. And Jace and Clary would gladly claim the title for themselves. All the more reason for them to appreciate the Clave and the Law: It's significantly more satisfying to kick a wall than it is to kick thin air. For the rebellious teen—or the teen who wants to feel like a rebel—a clearly defined law gives you something to define yourself against.

If you're looking to fight a war, it helps to have an enemy.

The beauty of Clave Law is that it allows you to feel like a rebel without actually doing much of anything rebellious—because when *everything* is legislated, breaking even the smallest of rules can offer the satisfaction of defiance without the consequences. "Isabelle only likes dating thoroughly inappropriate boys our parents will hate," Alec says in *City of Glass.* "Mundanes, Downworlders, petty crooks." The operative word here is "petty," because that's exactly what Isabelle's so-called rebellions are. In fact, it's hard not to suspect that the commitment-phobic Isabelle is dating these inappropriate boys precisely because she knows exactly how far things can go with them: far enough to feel like she's flirting with trouble, but never so far that she'd have to introduce her new werewolf fiancé to Mom and Dad. It's the perfect excuse to keep relationships skin deep—because any cute Downworlder might be worth bending the rules for, but who could be worth breaking them for? And so she gets to harmlessly test her boundaries, feeling like a proud rebel, while still protecting her heart. The same goes for our other heroes. Like prep school kids defiling a school uniform, the teen Shadowhunters get to call themselves rebels for the smallest of infractions: sneaking out, dating the wrong people. But when it comes to the big stuff? Even Jace, who has the most flagrant disregard for the Law, especially when it comes to Clary (after all, this is a guy who's not only willing to Mark an ostensible mundane but is also pretty open to the idea of sleeping with his sister), turns into a total priss. Remember his horror at Madame

Dorothea's failure to bend to the will of the Shadowhunters: "You knew there were Forsaken in this house and you didn't notify [the Clave]? Just the existence of Forsaken is a crime against the Covenant" (*City of Bones*). Jace sounds like a class prefect taking someone to task for running in the halls, and, like the class delinquent, Madame Dorothea practically laughs in his face.

Admittedly, as the trilogy continues, Clary and co.'s rule-breaking becomes more daring and more flagrant—their rebellions become quite a bit less petty. Jace presides over Simon's burial and awakening and later saves the young vampire with an emergency infusion of his own blood; Alec breaks Jace out of the Inquisitor's prison; Jace tries to pay it forward by breaking Simon out of the Gard. They're lawbreakers, no question: serious rebels. But their rebellions are almost always against specific edicts laid down by members of the Clave—against the bad (and often, in terms of the Law, illegal) decisions of individuals. They rebel against the man...while maintaining their absolute respect for the institution.

At no point do any of our characters, even Clary—the newcomer who could be expected to poke holes in the establishment—bother to question the fundamental tenets of Shadowhunter life. No one, for example, questions Luke's expulsion from the Shadowhunter ranks or suggests that he be readmitted (in whatever capacity he could fight at their side), even if he is a werewolf. No one (until the end of the first three books) questions the sharp divisions and political imbalance between Shadowhunters and Downworlders; no one questions the wisdom of keeping all this secret from the mundanes; no one questions the rules of who's in charge and what the penalties are for disobeying. These are the kinds of questions that *Valentine* liked to ask. Also known as: unthinkable. As it's unthinkable for Isabelle to imagine challenging the Clave's (and her parents') stance on homosexuality: If they discovered that Alec was gay, she says, they'd disown him, because that's just the way it works—of course, as we discover, the Lightwoods aren't so ready as their daughter believes to toss away their son based on an outmoded tradition. But Isabelle assumes they will be, and that "there's nothing I can do" (*City of Bones*).

The Tyranny of Choice

> *"My oath to the Covenant binds me."*
> —Jace Wayland, *City of Bones*

There's nothing I can do. It's a constant Shadowhunter refrain.

It's also a comforting lie, and the biggest reason of all why someone might be tempted to cling to a system of Laws and absolutes—a system that narrows your choices down to one.

In *The Paradox of Choice*, a book about why the proliferation of choice has made modern Americans increasingly unhappy, psychologist Barry Schwartz argues that the more choices we have, the more opportunity there is for confusion, paralysis, and regret: "As the number of choices keep growing, negative aspects of having a multitude of options begin to appear. As the number of choices grows further, the negatives escalate until we become overloaded. At this point, choice no longer liberates, but debilitates. It might even be said to tyrannize."

In other words: Choosing for yourself is hard, especially when none of the choices is particularly appealing.

Submitting to something like the Clave, an institution that makes your decisions for you, means abdicating the responsibility of choice and so escaping its consequences.

In *City of Bones*, Clary wants to know: Does Jace really believe it's right to kill someone in revenge? Jace replies by citing the Law—"A Shadowhunter who kills another of his brothers is worse than a demon and should be put down like one"—and offers this reply "sounding as if he were reciting the words from a textbook." Faced with a thorny moral predicament, he doesn't even have to think; the Clave does his thinking for him.

It's not just the consequences of action that the Law saves you from—it's the consequence of being yourself. It's no surprise that of all the characters, Alec is the one with the most knee-jerk fealty to Shadowhunter Law and tradition—even though he is the one with the most to lose. Alec clings to the Law as a shield to hide behind. He can't be himself, he can't accept his true feelings, he can't pursue the one he loves, not because he's afraid (or so he tells himself), but because the Law forbids it. (Funny, then, that when he's inscribed with the Fearless rune, he's suddenly ready to shout the truth to the world.) Clary, hewing for once to a higher law, complains that she can't be held responsible for her feelings or her actions because all that is inconsequential in the face of love: "When you love someone, you don't have a choice...Love takes your choices away" (*City of Ashes*).

They may be using the concept of law for opposite purposes, but Clary and Alec are both taking refuge in the same fantasy of compulsion. They can't be held responsible for themselves; they have no choice. For Clary, it's love that decides for her, so she can't be held accountable for her feelings; for Alec, it's the Law that forces him to deny his feelings. But in both cases, they're driven by the same fear: What might happen if they decided for themselves?

"[T]his is how the Clave works," Alec reminds Jace in *City of Glass*, when the new Inquisitor lays claim to Simon, supposedly for the purpose of getting him safely back home. "We don't get to control everything that happens. But you have to trust them, because otherwise everything turns into chaos." Things in Idris have gotten scary, they've gotten *real*, and there are real lives at stake—including Simon's. Yes, over the course of two books, Alec and the others have proven their courage and their willingness to take the initiative in a crisis and save the day. But they've done so through necessity, stepping up in case of emergency because there was no one else. Now, Alec implies, they can go back to what they were supposed to be doing: playing the obedient, pliable children, letting the grown-ups take over and fix things. Letting the grown-ups make the hard decisions (and then take the blame if and when everything goes to hell).

Alec says *we don't* get *to control everything that happens*— but he means *we don't* have to *control everything that happens.*

It's a child's strategy; it's a coward's excuse. And so it takes a coward to point out that it's time to grow up. In the face of Clary's despair over the probable loss of everything that matters to her, Amatis Herondale tells her exactly what she's doing wrong and sets the stage for the first trilogy's triumphant climax: "Oh, Clary. Don't you see? There's *always* something you can do. It's just people like me who always tell themselves otherwise" (*City of Glass*). It's a pivotal moment for the book, and for Clary. She's been inching toward this realization herself—all those minor rebellions and impertinent questions and treasonous authorities and "inevitable" injustices surely adding up to *something*—but it's Amatis who pushes her over the brink. It's Amatis who aims a spotlight at the terrifying truth Clary hasn't wanted to see. It's terrifying because fatalism is easy. Surrender is easy. Taking charge of your own life and your choices, no matter how ugly things get? That can be hard enough to seem impossible.

By the end of *City of Glass*, Clary is ready for the impossible. With Amatis' charge ringing in her ears, with the Clave ready to throw up its hands and give in to Valentine, with all hope apparently lost, Clary is done letting other people tell her what she can and cannot do. And after hundreds of pages of excuses, of *there's nothing I can do* and *the Law is the Law*, finally, someone stands up to say *there's something I can do.*

There's a choice after all.

There's always a choice.

This is the lesson our heroes need to embrace before they can grow up…and before they can triumph. To win, they need to do more than just question the rules. They need to *change* them. The runes of the past aren't enough to win a battle against Valentine's demon army, but if Clary and co. break the rules? If they write a *new* rune, and write it across the skin of every Shadowhunter, if they incite an entire society to buck the established order, if only for a single day, they just might prevail. It's the key to defeating Valentine, but it's also the key to their coming of age—to Alec embracing his identity, to Jace choosing his true family, to Clary discovering her inner warrior. Before any of that can happen, they need to reject the comfort they've found in following the rules and letting someone else call the shots. They need to understand their lives aren't prescribed and predetermined, that things don't need to work the way they always have, that the future is unwritten and belongs to them. No matter how terrifying, they need to decide that the only rules that matter are the ones they write themselves.

Robin Wasserman *is the author of several books for children and young adults, including the Cold Awakening Trilogy,* Hacking Harvard, *and, most recently,* The Book of Blood and Shadow. *She lives and writes (and occasionally procrastinates) in Brooklyn. You can find more information about her and her books at www.robinwasserman.com.*

When I read Michelle's essay for the first time, I was stuck between wanting to dance around in delight and wanting to have a good sympathy cry. It was a complicated feeling, as you can see. She's clearly done her research, and it shows in this detailed exploration of Simon's two kinds of Otherness: being Jewish, and being a vampire. I feel I have no words that can do this essay justice, except to say that I'm so, so glad it was written.

I'll end with a quote from below: "[Simon] demonstrates more than any other character in the Mortal Instruments that it is not our blood but our actions that define who we are."

Sniff.

SIMON LEWIS: JEWISH, VAMPIRE, HERO

iddle:
We have existed for centuries. Our days begin at night. We can't eat what our neighbors eat. Who are we?

Answer:
If you guessed "Jews," you would be right.

If you guessed "vampires," you would also be right.

And if you guessed "Jewish vampires," you would be thinking of Simon Lewis.

Jews and Vampires as "Other"

Historically, the Jewish people are culturally "Other," a minority that has existed for centuries despite plenty of persecution and comprising less than 0.2 percent of the world's population. We are a nomadic people, in exile from the Jewish homeland since before the common era. But despite our long history of persecution, despite our tiny numbers, despite the fact that those numbers are spread all over the world in the Diaspora (more literally translated as exile)—despite all of this, the Jewish people have remained virtually unchanged for millennia. Jews still eat matzo, unleavened bread, on Passover in Bangkok and Tel Aviv. On Rosh Hashanah, the Jewish New Year, a ram's horn, the *shofar*, is still blown in synagogues in Fiji and Finland. The Jewish people have fasted on Yom Kippur, the Day of Atonement, since before Christianity existed. Civilizations rise and fall, but the Jewish people still exist, a wandering nation among nations. The world may change, but we remain.

As a people, Jews have cultural, religious, and behavioral restrictions, obligations, codes, and standards of conduct that set us apart from the rest of the world. The Torah and Talmud codify laws that govern every moment of a Jewish person's day throughout every stage of life, from morning until night, from birth until death. Our days begin and end at sundown; the Sabbath, for example, begins at sundown on Friday night and continues until sundown on Saturday night—not Sunday. And perhaps most famously, we are prohibited from eating foods that aren't kosher, including a litany of foods recounted in Leviticus. Pork and shellfish are the most well known of those foods, but we're also forbidden from consuming blood, whether it comes from a kosher animal or not. When a kosher animal, such as a cow, is slaughtered according to Jewish law, the meat must be drained of blood through the liberal application of salt so that we don't ingest a single drop. According to Leviticus 17:10:

> And whatsoever man there be of the house of Israel, or of the strangers that sojourn among them, that eateth any manner of blood, I will set My face against that soul that eateth blood, and will cut him off from among his people.

And yet we have been accused throughout history of drinking human blood. The first instances of blood libel leveled against the Jewish people were recorded in the eleventh century and were immortalized in a ballad depicting the ritual murder of the child Hugh of England in 1255.[1] In the Middle Ages, not practicing Christianity was thought to be evidence of devil worship, and attempts were made to wipe out entire Jewish communities. Accusing us of drinking the blood of Christian children was a surefire, inflammatory way of prejudicing non-Jewish neighbors against us. Rumors also grew that Jews could reanimate after death, so naturally Jewish corpses were burned or decapitated and staked for good measure.

---

[1] Rabbi Ken Spiro, "History Crash Course #46: Blood Libel," accessed June 25, 2012, www.aish.com/jl/h/cc/48951151.html. Alan Dundes, *The Blood Libel: A Case in Anti-Semitic Folklore.*

In the nineteenth century, there was no Other as culturally frightening as the Jew. Most often emigrating from eastern Europe, Jewish people were depicted as paleskinned, black-clothed, hook-nosed, and sunken-eyed. As immigrants, we were rootless—wanderers, with no national identity—but nevertheless seen as clannish. Jews reject the cross and holy water. We did business and engaged with our adoptive nations, but we resisted assimilation, prompting allegations of parasitism, of feeding off those host countries like leeches and ticks and lice (which is how much anti-Semitic propaganda depicts us). And one of Hitler's personal inspirations, Karl Lueger, a mayor of Vienna, was known to have tossed off the term *blutsauger* in reference to Jews. The translation: bloodsucker.

One popular theory about Bram Stoker's Dracula, the vampire standard-bearer, is that he was a monstrous, Gothic incarnation of these anti-Semitic stereotypes: a hooknosed, wealthy wanderer of eastern European origins with a lust for blood and wealth. Think such hatefulness and ignorance is in the past? Think again. As recently as 2010, a cartoon run on the Al Aqsa children's channel of the terrorist group Hamas portrayed anti-Semitic stereotypes of Orthodox Jews drinking the blood of Muslim children.[2] Blood libel and anti-Semitism, which helped fuel the atrocities of

---

[2] "New Antisemitic Animated Film Vilifies the Palestinian Authority—PA Security Forces Help Stereotypical Blood-Drinking Jews," accessed June 25, 2012, www.liveleak.com/view?i=ca3_1262544454. Chris Spags, "New Hamas Cartoon Features Blood-Drinking Jews, Other Fun," accessed June 25, 2012, http://guyism.com/entertainment/tv/new-hamas-cartoon-features-blood-drinking-jews-other-fun.html.

the Crusades and the Inquisition and the Holocaust, are clearly still alive and well in the twenty-first century.

Though the image of the Jewish people has remained virtually unchanged through time, the image of the vampire has not. Vampires aren't entirely the same today as they were in the era of Nosferatu and Dracula; see *True Blood* and *Twilight* and more books and films and television shows than I can name. Still, a few things remain: Typically they are depicted as pale-skinned, sunlight-shunning undead who need blood to survive. In the Mortal Instruments series, vampires belong to clans. They are immortal. They are vulnerable to holy symbols, though which ones depend on individual vampires' beliefs. They are pale. They are nocturnal. They can shape-shift into bats and dust and rats, and they can control and mesmerize humans. They have laws and rituals and needs that differentiate them from other classes of Downworlders, often in unflattering ways.

Because of the historically anti-Semitic associations between Jews and vampires, portraying even a fictional Jew as a vampire, a blood drinker, could go dangerously awry. The Jewish people may even today still embody the cultural Other, but monsters, we aren't.

Technically, though, Simon Lewis *is*. Clary Fray, Mortal Instruments' heroine, is a Shadowhunter; so is Jace Wayland, the hero. Their mission? To protect mundanes from Downworlders. Monsters. Which is exactly what Simon becomes.

Or does he?

The Everyman as the Other

We first meet Simon Lewis at New York City's Pandemonium Club, which he attends with Clary. She notes that he stands out in the sea of dyed/pierced/adventurously dressed teenagers because he looks so *normal*. Freshly scrubbed hair, check. Glasses, check. Lovably nerdy T-shirt, check. "[A]s if he were on his way to chess club" (*City of Bones*), Clary says. (Oh, Simon.)

In the chapters that follow, there are references to Simon's Jewishness aplenty, couched in his trademark self-deprecating humor. But despite Simon's status as a member of the "other" tribe, he almost seems to function in the narrative of *City of Bones* as the Everyman: the average sidekick to Clary Fray's powerful heroine, the nice cute guy to Jace Wayland's sexy bad boy. He is so normal, so *mundane*, that even the other characters are prompted to ask what Simon is still doing at the New York Institute post–demon attack shenanigans, long after he should have been kicked out. He is singled out as Other not because he is different from us, the readers, but because, in being normal, he is different from the other characters, and therefore doesn't belong.

It would be forgivable to wonder why, then, with the spotlight necessarily following Clary as she works through her litany of protagonist's problems (Demons! Missing parents! Strange gifts!), it is stated more than once that Simon-the-sidekick is Jewish. Token minority syndrome is a not-uncommon character affliction, one in which a secondary character seems to belong to a cultural/ethnic/religious minority solely as a means to set him or her apart from other secondary characters. And when presented with an ensemble that includes as disparate and remarkable a cast as Clary, Jace, Valentine Morgenstern, Alec and Isabelle Lightwood, Magnus Bane—you get the picture—you could be forgiven for wondering if perhaps Simon's Jewish identity was thrown in just to make him stand out a *little*.

But then things change. As they always do.

The Other versus the Other: The Vampire versus the Jew

After Simon is attacked at the Hotel Dumont in *City of Ashes*, Raphael, the leader of the New York vampire clan, appears at the Institute holding Simon's bloody, alternately limp or writhing body in his arms, and presents the Shadowhunters with a choice: Kill Simon or help him transform into a vampire. A Downworlder. A monster. The very thing that Shadowhunters are meant to protect mundanes like Simon against.

To put it mildly, it's not an easy choice, and Simon, while writhing and all, is incapable of making it himself. So Jace asks Clary what Simon would want, if he could choose. When Clary speaks, she is clear—they can bury him to help him rise as a vampire, but she will be there when it happens. And she insists that he be buried in a Jewish cemetery.

Simon is blood-soaked and suffering, and the longer the Shadowhunters wait, the higher the likelihood that he will die. But even though time is of the essence, Clary doesn't order everyone to take Simon to the *nearest* cemetery—she insists that it be a *Jewish* cemetery. Clary, who knows Simon better than anyone, knows that being Jewish is an inextricable part of his identity, so she makes the choice she knows he would make for himself. In making that demand, she is making a statement. A big one.

The laws surrounding death and burial are yet another way that the Jewish people have remained distinct, separate, and Other from the cultures and civilizations around them. As the Roman historian Tacitus wrote in his *Histories*, "The Jews bury rather than burn their dead," distinguishing us, the Jews, from them, the Romans. There are strict procedures that govern the watching, the washing, and the guarding of the body when a Jewish person dies, far too numerous and complicated to recount. They comprise volumes of the Talmud (oral law) and Torah (written law). As the young Shadowhunters discover, so too are there strict procedures that govern the burial and subsequent rising of a vampire, and they enact them under Raphael's guidance.

When Simon emerges from the earth, he is chillingly transformed. And when he is offered blood, Clary watches as "Simon, who had been a vegetarian since he was ten years old…snatched the packet of blood out of Raphael's thin brown hand and tore into it with his teeth" (*City of Ashes*). The only thing Simon wants and needs in his first moments as a vampire is blood. And his first act as a vampire is to violate Jewish law—in a Jewish cemetery, no less.

It's a masterful metaphor. In becoming a vampire, Simon becomes Other in ways that clearly parallel but are fundamentally incompatible with Judaism. He finds himself a member of a tribe governed by laws—but he is loath to abide them. He finds his diet restricted and regulated—but he is loath to satisfy his new needs. Simon's new identity as a vampire immediately conflicts with and encroaches on his identity as a Jew, one of the most defining characteristics of his human life. Simon has always been different and Other from the Shadowhunters, but as a vampire, he is now Other in a new and sinister way.

Unfortunately for him, it's only the beginning.

As *City of Ashes* progresses, Simon struggles to remain himself despite the physical ways in which vampirism transforms him. He nearly singes his fingers when he places them in the sunlight for the first time. His every waking and slumbering moment is consumed by the thought of and thirst for blood. But, as he says, "At least Jace can't call me *mundane* anymore."

Indeed, after he rises, Simon Lewis is no longer mundane. But his supernatural transformation doesn't bring him closer to Clary's world; it pushes him farther away from it. No one needs to tease Simon about not belonging in the Institute anymore; after becoming a vampire, he physically can no longer enter it. As Clary thinks, "Simon would never see the inside of a church or a synagogue again."

This is another indication of the obstacles Simon faces in retaining his Jewish identity, but it isn't the last. Simon's status as a vampire not only prevents him from entering into his house of worship; it prevents him from verbalizing that worship too. Valentine takes Simon prisoner and, just before he is about to die, asks him for any last words: "Simon knew what he was supposed to say. *Sh'ma Yisrael, adonai elohanu, adonai echod.* Hear, oh Israel, the Lord our God, the Lord is One. He tried to speak the words, but a searing pain burned his throat" (*City of Ashes*).

Those words that Simon desperately wants to speak but, as a vampire, cannot, are the most famous lines in Judaism, called the Shema. The Torah instructs Jews to teach the words of the Shema to our children, to recite them in our morning prayers when we wake, and to take care that they are the last words we utter each night before we sleep (Deuteronomy 6:6, 6:7). The words of the Shema were spoken by Moses in his farewell to the Jewish people, and they were spoken by Jews before entering gas chambers during the Holocaust. They are a pledge of allegiance to God, the ultimate declaration of faith, and even though Simon's unwanted, immutable status as a vampire prevented him from declaring them, he *wanted* to. He clung to his faith, his Jewish identity, even then.

And not for the last time. In *City of Glass*, when the Clave is in the process of investigating why and how Simon became a Daylighter, they throw him in prison in Alicante, accusing him of being Valentine's spy. Wondering if he can escape, Simon touches the bars, but his flesh is singed:

> He realized now that not all the runes were runes at all: Carved between them were Stars of David and lines from the Torah in Hebrew. The carvings looked new.
>
> *The guards were here half the day talking about how to keep you penned in*, the voice had said.
>
> But it hadn't just been because he was a vampire, laughably; it had partly been because he was Jewish. They had spent half the day carving the Seal of Solomon into that doorknob so it would burn him when he touched it. It had taken them this long to turn the articles of his faith against him.
>
> For some reason the realization stripped away the last of Simon's self-possession. He sank down onto the bed and put his head in his hands.

If Simon were to cast aside his Jewish identity and beliefs, the Seal of Solomon, the Star of David, and the lines from the Torah couldn't be used against him as a vampire—they would be useless, and he could be free. In his new form, bound by new physical laws, Simon the Vampire is more vulnerable if he clings to his identity as Simon the Jew than if he were to forsake it. But even though his identity as a vampire threatens to erode his Jewish identity, and even though his status as a believer now can (and does) harm him, he nevertheless holds fast to it. In doing so, Clare evokes a powerful connection between Simon, who has been forcefully, unwillingly transformed into a vampire yet maintains his Jewish faith, and his Jewish ancestors, many of whom faced forced conversions (and executions) but practiced their faith in cellars and attics and cattle cars and prisons, during sieges and the Crusades and the Inquisition and the Holocaust. Simon's retention of his Jewish beliefs and identity in the face of circumstances in which it would behoove him, help him, to give them up echoes the Jewish people's ability not only to endure and to survive but to *believe* in the face of persecution, even when it would be easier to let go.

Valentine seems to find this notion absurd, especially given that Simon is a Downworlder. He laughs upon realizing that Simon choked on the name of God—the very idea that Simon, a "monster," the Other, would still believe in and invoke God is ridiculous to him. He views Simon as a monster who doesn't understand that he *is* one and then attempts to kill Simon for his Otherness even though Simon doesn't behave as, associate with, or identify with other vampires. Valentine doesn't care—his perception of the "impurity" of Simon's blood (also a familiar anti-Semitic claim) is all that matters to him. But his attempt to purge Simon from the world backfires. When Jace saves Simon's life by allowing him to drink Jace's blood, it transforms him into a Daylighter who can't be killed or harmed by sunlight the way every other vampire can. Simon becomes unique even among his new, acquired culture, Other even among his own adoptive kind, and it forces him into exile, like the first wanderer, Cain.

Exile and the Mark of Cain

In *City of Glass*, the mundane who was barely worth acknowledging finds himself at the center of the Mortal War, with multiple sides jockeying for the advantage that he, Simon the Daylighter, would bring them. That status makes him uniquely desirable but also uniquely vulnerable, so to protect him Clary Marks him with a rune she has seen in her vision.

Multiple characters discuss the possibility that Cain, the first child born on earth, became the bearer of the first Mark because he murdered his brother, Abel. In *City of Ashes*, Magnus even quotes from the Torah, "And the Lord said unto him, Therefore whosoever slayeth Cain, vengeance shall be taken on him sevenfold. And the Lord set a Mark upon Cain, lest any finding him should kill him." But in order to understand the significance of Cain's mark, it helps first to understand the circumstances in which it was bestowed upon him.

According to Genesis, Cain brings a sacrifice, and his brother, Abel, brings one that is superior. God rejects Cain's sacrifice, and Cain's countenance falls. He's disappointed. Upset. God, seeing Cain's reaction, states: "Surely if you improve yourself, you will be forgiven. But if you do not improve yourself, sin rests at the door. Its desire is toward you, yet you can conquer it" (Genesis 4:7).

But Cain does not listen to God. He doesn't improve himself—far from it. He kills his brother out of envy and then lies about it to God. God, unsurprisingly, is not fooled: "The voice of your brother's blood cries out to me from the ground. Therefore you are cursed more than the ground which opens wide its mouth to receive your brother's blood from your hand. When you work the ground, it shall not open up its land to you. You shall become a vagrant and a wanderer" (Genesis 4:10–4:12).

The Jewish sage Tzor Hamor comments that now Cain "will know no more peace than his brother's blood." After hearing this, Cain begs for mercy: "Is my iniquity too great to be borne? To become a vagrant and a wanderer on earth, whoever meets me will kill me." Cain is asking, in essence, whether committing murder merits that *he* should die too. In answer, God grants Cain mercy. He bestows upon him the Mark, saying, "Whoever slays Cain before seven generations will be punished" (Genesis 4:15).

Simon wonders, in *City of Fallen Angels*, why he's saddled with this burden: "He wasn't Cain, who had killed his brother, but the curse believed he was." He thinks too, "That's part of the curse, isn't it? 'A fugitive and a wanderer shalt thou be.'" And *I* wondered why Simon still considers the Mark of Cain a "curse" when he did nothing to deserve it. After reading these passages in Genesis, though, I think I get it: Simon isn't like Cain because he killed his brother. He's like Cain because he *wants* to kill his brother—his metaphorical one, anyway. Part of Simon wants to drink human blood, to kill his brothers and sisters in humanity.

And part of him always will. "Sin rests at the door," God says to Cain. The Hebrew word for sin is *chet,* and it appears in reference to a slingshot that has missed its target. The Hebrew word for repentance is *teshuva,* which means, literally, "to return." In explaining God's response to Cain's inadequate sacrifice, the Jewish sage Sforno explains: "If you succumb to your evil inclination then punishment and evil will be as ever present as if they lived in your doorway."[3]

What's an evil inclination, you ask? The Jewish idea of the *Yetzer Hara* (evil inclination) exists in opposition to the *Yetzer HaTov* (positive inclination). Through no fault of his own, from the moment Simon was transformed into a vampire, he is tempted, as Cain was, to spill human blood—to kill those who were once his brothers and sisters in humanity. This *Yetzer Hara,* Simon's nonhuman, evil inclination, is in constant opposition to his moral aims: his *Yetzer HaTov,* his positive inclination. It tempts him to "miss" his target, to stray from his beliefs and identity as a Jew and as a former human. In an argument with werewolf (and potential love interest) Maia Roberts, she calls him a monster, and "Some part of him wanted to fight her, to wrestle her down and puncture her skin with his teeth, to gulp her hot blood. The rest of him felt as if it were screaming" (*City of Ashes*).

It is right after he muses about the nature of his curse at the beginning of *City of Fallen Angels* that Simon, who has so far managed to stave off his thirst, his inclination to kill, succumbs to temptation and attacks Maureen. Before this, before Simon sins and "misses" his target in such a major,

---

[3] Rabbi Nosson Scherman, *The Torah: Haftaros and Five Megillos with a Commentary Anthologized from the Rabbinic Writings (The Stone Edition).*

unalterable way, he arguably doesn't deserve to be a fugitive and a wanderer—the "curse" of the Mark of Cain, as he views it. So before he attacks Maureen, what has Simon done to warrant the terrible, damning mercy of the Mark? Is it an injustice?

I don't think it is. I think—even though Simon doesn't yet—that the Mark *itself* isn't his curse; the Mark isn't what makes him a fugitive, a wanderer in exile. So what does?

His refusal to assimilate.

Cultural Assimilation

There are benefits to being a vampire in the Shadowhunters' world. Immortality. Beauty. Strength. Community.

But Simon rejects that community. He rejects vampire ideals by not relishing his vampire status. He consumes blood to stay alive—but only animal blood. He tries to hide the truth from his mother—because he is ashamed and in denial about what he has become. And perhaps most tellingly, Simon resists interacting with other vampires. He doesn't live with them. He doesn't feed with them. He doesn't befriend them. He behaves more like vampirism is a disease he *has*, rather than something that defines who and what he *is*. He does not see himself as being one of *them*.

But if he chose to, he could be.

When Simon finally acknowledges and proves to his mother that he is a vampire in *City of Fallen Angels*, she calls him a monster and casts him out of his own home. That devastates him, to the point that he actually asks Raphael if he can stay at the Hotel Dumont—with those who initially turned him into the thing that he hates. It's a request of last resort—Simon literally feels like he has nowhere else to go, having been kicked out of his mundane home and being unable to enter the Institute with his friends. But as Raphael says, "In every way you do not accept what you really are, and as long as that is true, you are not welcome at the Dumont." Camille Belcourt, another vampire, says to Simon, "You befriend Shadowhunters, but you can never be of them. You will always be other and outside."

The primary authority figures in Simon's new, adoptive culture—vampire culture—express disdain at his refusal to assimilate, to acculturate to their ways. Raphael takes the position that Simon is in denial about his true nature—that his humanity (his positive inclination, his *Yetzer HaTov,* of which Jewish identity is a significant part) is gone. Camille attempts a subtler, more subversive pressure; she doesn't deny Simon's humanity—she appeals to it. To his yearning to belong and to his feeling of loneliness with infinity stretching out before him. But even Camille then mocks his inability to speak the name of God, saying that if he were to simply abandon his beliefs, the name of God would lack meaning and he could speak it without a problem.

Simon ultimately rejects her and Raphael both. He is unwilling to abandon his Jewish identity, his humanity, his *Yetzer HaTov,* even though it means forgoing community. Even though it means remaining separate and Other from Downworlders and Shadowhunters still. In his staunch refusal to assimilate into vampire culture—despite the benefits it affords, despite how harmonious it would doubtless feel to not have to constantly struggle with his *Yetzer Hara,* or vampirism, if he were to truly identify and live as one of them—Simon embodies the commitment of the Jewish people to adhere to the core beliefs and traditions that have made us separate, distinct, and Other from every other culture for centuries and for millennia.

It is a fundamentally Jewish act.

Simon is a denizen of two worlds—the Downworlders' and the mundane world. But while he *can't* be a part of the mundane world anymore, he *chooses* not to belong in the Downworlders'. He is a wanderer not because of the Mark of Cain, not because he is "cursed." He is in exile because he *chooses* to be. Simon would rather belong nowhere than belong with other vampires; he would rather be nothing than be the creature ruled by his *Yetzer Hara*, the animalistic instinct we glimpsed in that Jewish cemetery.

In *City of Glass*, Valentine says to Simon:

> "I've seen you choke on the name of God, vampire…As for why you can stand in the sunlight—"
> he broke off and grinned. "You're an anomaly, perhaps. A freak. But still a monster."

Simon is a freak among freaks, Valentine says. A monster among monsters, who can't even speak the name of God. But here is a character who was transformed into a predator that *has* to harm others to survive, and still he wrestles with his "evil inclination," his instinct to kill and drink blood. The Jewish concept that sin rests always at the door is truer for no one than it is for Simon. But despite how he suffers in *City of Fallen Angels*—despite the fact that he is tested and fails (with Maureen), missing his target spectacularly—Simon refuses to accept that being a vampire is what he *is*. He doesn't let his Downworlder blood define him and embraces belief instead, even though doing so cuts him off from those who most closely resemble what he has become.

Perhaps it's the Jewish will to survive and endure, to persist unchanging in our beliefs despite the most horrific circumstances, that lends Simon the strength to survive and endure and hold onto his Jewish identity and humanity, to embrace his moral aims even as a new, dark, intruding part of him urges him to let go. But whatever the source, in fighting to retain that humanity, Simon proves that despite being a vampire, he isn't a monster at all.

He proves that he's a hero.

The Other as the Hero

In *City of Bones*, Simon is a mundane whom virtually no one bothers to talk to because he doesn't matter—he is Other because he is painfully normal. But in *City of Lost Souls*, the world, and Jace's life, hangs in the balance—and Simon is seemingly the only one who can save it. The Clave would kill Jace if they found him—not because they're evil, but because they believe the greater good is served in saving the lives of many over the life of one. To stop them and to help Jace, Simon bargains using the only chip he's got—himself.

Despite the fact that Magnus is clear about not being able to guarantee Simon's safety, Simon decides to call on the angel Raziel himself in order to procure a weapon that would separate Jace from Sebastian without killing him. "I'm not Nephilim…I can't do what [Jace] can do," he says to Isabelle, justifying to her and himself why he should be willing to sacrifice his life for the chance to save Jace's.

When Simon raises Raziel, it brings him face-to-face with death again. "This time he did not try to say the words, only thought them. Hear, O Israel! The Lord is our God, the Lord is one—" Simon doesn't die, but what's notable is that what saves him is the Mark of Cain—the very thing Simon considers a curse. It prevents Raziel from taking his life and enables him to request the sword.

As the Angel tells him, "You would kill the one and preserve the other. Easiest of course to simply kill both." But Simon refuses to accept this, even from an Angel. "I know we're not much compared to you, but we don't kill our friends. We try to save them. If Heaven didn't want it that way, we ought never have been given the ability to love."

Simon has no special love for Jace, nor Jace for Simon, as all fellow devourers of the Mortal Instruments series know, but Simon decides to save Jace anyway—not for himself, or for Clary, or for the world, but because he believes it is the *right thing to do*. It's a brave, bold move, arguing with an Angel, and it doesn't go unnoticed. "A veritable warrior of your people, like him whose name you bear, Simon Maccabeus," the Angel says. He then agrees to provide Simon with the sword—at the cost of his Mark.

Simon hates the Mark. It scares him. But deep down, Simon also thinks it's "the thing that made him special." Not one thing—*the* thing. The only thing.

And still, Simon lets it go.

It is a sacrifice, relinquishing the Mark's protection, and it's only after he makes it that Raziel calls him "Simon Maccabeus"—which is not, as Simon helpfully informs him, his name. It is Raziel, however, who then corrects Simon: "But you are of the blood and faith of the Maccabees. Some say the Maccabees were Marked by the hand of God. In either case you are a warrior of heaven, Daylighter, whether you like it or not" (*City of Lost Souls*).

Simon Maccabeus, the youngest of the five Maccabean brothers, made a tactical and strategic alliance that prompted the full independence of Judea, and under his reign, the Jewish people became politically autonomous for the first time since the era of the First Temple. He won wars and led his people into one of the most prosperous periods in Jewish history.

On the surface, it seems like Simon still has a long way to go before he earns the title "warrior." But a deeper look reveals that Simon has been fighting a war since *City of Ashes*—the war between the positive and evil inclinations, the *Yetzer HaTov* and *Yetzer Hara*, that rages inside him every second of every day of his vampire existence. Physically he may be more demon than human, but he is called a warrior of *heaven* by an *Angel,* no less.

From the moment Simon is changed into a vampire, he is transformed into the Gothic Other; something inhuman, something *else*. And because of it, like Cain, the desire to kill, the desire to sin, rests at his door. If Simon gave in, he would be physically stronger. If he accepted Camille's offer of "community," he would be less lonely. If he abandoned his Jewish beliefs, he would be less vulnerable as a vampire. Simon could rationalize each of those decisions—he didn't *choose* to become a vampire, he is what he is, it isn't his fault, et cetera.

But he never does.

Simon Lewis isn't perfect. He sins. He "misses." He is tempted in *City of Fallen Angels*, and even though he isn't a literal angel, he certainly does fall. But in *City of Lost Souls*, despite his mother's rejection and his wandering and his loneliness, despite flirting with the idea of giving up and giving in, Simon returns to himself. He never let go of the things that make him *Simon*: his Jewish identity, his beliefs. He sinned—he missed the mark—but he returns. And in returning, he shines.

Not because he was born a Shadowhunter, like Alec and Isabelle, and not because the blood of angels runs through his veins, as it does for Clary and Jace. He wasn't born to be a hero the way they were. But in holding on to his humanity throughout the physical metamorphosis that threatens to swallow it, he demonstrates more than any other character in the Mortal Instruments that it is not our blood but our *actions* that define who we are. And when Simon finally realizes this about himself, he finds that, for the first time since he was changed, he is able to speak the name of God.

Michelle Hodkin grew up in Florida, went to college in New York, and studied law in Michigan. Like Simon, she is Jewish. Unlike Simon, she is not a vampire. When she isn't writing about Jewish vampires or ill-behaved teenagers in her books The Unbecoming of Mara Dyer *(Simon & Schuster BFYR, 2011),* The Evolution of Mara Dyer *(Simon & Schuster BFYR, 2012), and* The Retribution of Mara Dyer *(Simon & Schuster BFYR, 2013), she can usually be found prying strange objects from the jaws of one of her three pets. You can visit her online at www.michellehodkin.com.*

After reading this essay, I've decided my writing doesn't get lumped in with the films of John Hughes often enough. I'll have to work on this.

Meanwhile, enjoy Kami's loving dissection of why the hapless best friends never get the girl...unless they happen to be the girl. But you'll read more about that in a minute.

Why the Best Friend Never Gets the Girl

I'm just going to come right out and say it because we're friends, and I don't want there to be any secrets between us (unless, of course, I'm your best friend and I'm madly in love with you). Brace yourself, here it comes: Simon never stood a chance with Clary.

Before you start sending hate mail, give me a chance to explain. I'm not suggesting that Simon isn't handsome and brave and perfect for Clary in every way. Some mundanes might actually argue that he's superior to Jace in all three categories, but that doesn't change the fundamental law of attraction on which my claim is based. *In literature and film, the best friend never gets the girl.*

It has nothing to do with Simon's potential as boyfriend material. He lost the battle before he even had a chance to fight, doomed to join support groups full of best friends who never got the girl. (The reverse is true if the person in question is a girl secretly in love with her best friend, but we'll get to that later.)

In pursuing Clary, Simon ignored a decade's worth of case studies conducted by a handful of gifted filmmakers in the 1980s, most notably John Hughes, the godfather of them all, who dedicated his career to exposing what I refer to as the Duckie effect.

For those of you unfamiliar with this master filmmaker and his legacy, the Duckie effect is this: A boy falls hopelessly in love with the girl of his dreams who also happens to be his best friend, spends all his time with her, yet she still chooses another guy over him. It's a fascinating and heartbreaking phenomenon, worthy of scientific research. But you don't need to be a scientist to analyze the data collected from the 1980s filmmakers and conclude that our Simon is a victim of the Duckie effect.

Case Study 1: Pretty in Pink *(John Hughes, 1986)*

It's only fitting to begin with the movie that includes the best friend after whom the phenomenon was named.

In *Pretty in Pink*, Andie is not one of the popular girls at her high school. In fact, she's one of their favorite targets. Andie wears the wrong clothes and drives a beat-up car, and she isn't the girl that most of the guys at her school want to date. Unless you happen to be Duckie, the guy who pretends he needs help with his homework just so he can spend time with her. Duckie is completely devoted to Andie, but she still falls for Blane, a handsome and popular guy at school—the complete opposite of Duckie in every way (sound familiar?). So what does Duckie do? He tries to make Andie jealous by kissing her friend Iona.

Exhibit A: *Like Duckie, Simon tries to make the girl he loves jealous.*

In *City of Bones*, Simon notices the attraction between Clary and Jace almost immediately and employs a slightly more sophisticated strategy to make Clary jealous. Simon focuses all his attention on the beautiful Isabelle, often staring at her "rapt and openmouthed." And he is actually more successful than Duckie. Simon does make Clary jealous, most notably at Magnus Bane's party, when she watches as Isabelle dances around Simon, "looking at him as if she were planning to drag him off into a corner to have sex." In American literature and film, consciously choosing a guy with whom they have an instant attraction is one of the ways young women signal their independence. Their sexual identities are closely tied to breaking free from their parents and the expectations others have for them—expectations that sometimes include a sweet best friend.

This might explain why making Clary jealous doesn't actually work in the long run. Jace is the one Clary is instantly attracted to and ultimately the one she wants—the aloof enigmatic boy who kisses her in the hallway outside her bedroom. Even when Simon interrupts the kiss and admits his feelings for Clary, professing "I've been in love with you for ten years," he still doesn't get the girl. Like Andie, Clary feels guilty and torn. But in the end, she can't fight the way she feels, and Jace wins out.

Case Study 2: Sixteen Candles *(John Hughes, 1984)*

Sixteen Candles is another example of the Duckie effect at work. In the film, Samantha is turning sixteen the same weekend her older sister is getting married. Relatives descend on the house, along with a foreign exchange student, and Sam loses her room and her family's attention. School is a welcome distraction, especially since her secret crush, Jake Ryan, is there.

Sam's "Duckie" is more of an accidental friend than a lifelong best friend. Farmer Ted, as Sam calls him, is king of the geeks, and he bets his friends that he can "make it" with Sam at the school dance. The same night, Sam's family forgets her sixteenth birthday. She shares a moment with Jake before his nightmare diva of a girlfriend drags him off to a party. Sam retreats to the school auto shop, where she spills her guts to best friend stand-in Farmer Ted and he tries to kiss her. Farmer Ted never gets a kiss (though Sam does give him her underwear so he can save face with his friends), and she ends up with Jake.

Farmer Ted and Simon have less in common than Duckie and Simon, since Farmer Ted isn't technically Sam's best friend. He does give Sam a shoulder to cry on and throws her an emotional life preserver when she needs one. But anyone who has ever harbored a monster crush knows a shoulder to cry on is no match for hundreds of class periods spent combining your name and your crush's (especially if you added his last name to your first name just to "see how it would look"). This is particularly true of young women in literature and film, who suffer extreme cases of the grass always being greener on the other side.

They seem to be more interested in the unattainable than in the boy who's busy adding his last name to theirs.

Exhibit B: Simon is the grass on this side—the known quantity.

Simon is the boy Clary confesses her hopes and fears to in the auto shop, not the boy whose name she writes over and over in class—or, in the case of Shadowhunters, the boy upon whose skin she draws runes.

Clary isn't the only one who needs an emotional life preserver. In *City of Bones*, Simon admits (though Clary denies it), "I've always been the one who needed you more than you needed me."

This brings up another important distinction between Duckies and guys who get the girls: The guy who gets the girl avoids showing both physical and emotional vulnerability, except to the one girl hc cares about.

Exhibit C: Jace bleeds and battles demons and still has enough energy to make a smartass comment afterward, while Simon just bleeds.

Unlike Simon, Jace doesn't seem to lean on anyone. He suffers silently, hiding the pain of losing his parents, his insecurities, even his feelings for Clary at first. As the series continues, we learn Jace's secrets along with Clary, and discover that he is more vulnerable than we could've imagined, which only makes him even more wounded and irresistible. To their detriment, Duckies are never wounded and irresistible (physically wounded maybe, but that's not quite as sexy).

Case Study 3: St. Elmo's Fire (Joel Schumacher and Carl Kurlander, 1985)

Another common denominator best friends in film and literature share is pining. You know, silently brooding over the girl you're madly in love with year after year without saying a word.

The ultimate case study in best friend pining is Kevin, Andrew McCarthy's character in the movie *St. Elmo's Fire*. In the film, seven best friends graduate from college, and their lives slowly fall apart, tearing their friendship apart along with them. Almost everyone in *St. Elmo's Fire* seems to have hooked up at some point, but Leslie and Alec are an actual couple. The turning point in the movie occurs when the lives of all seven of the characters are spinning out of control, and Leslie confronts Alec about his "extracurricular love life." Alec throws Leslie out of their apartment, and she ends up at her best friend Kevin's place.

They both drink too much, Leslie finds a box full of pictures Kevin has secretly snapped of her over the years (can anyone say stalker?), and Kevin admits that he's been in love with her since they met. But viewers know Kevin is in love with Leslie long before she figures it out. The way he seems uncomfortable when Leslie and Alec are together, the awkward glances and longing looks—it's all right there on the screen.

In the case of Simon, it's right there on the page as soon as the Mortal Instruments series begins.

Exhibit D: *Simon has been in love with Clary for years.*

The boy who gets the girl never pines. He kisses her in the hall and takes her breath away, or he kisses her in front of the Seelie Court, even when he thinks she's his sister (a fact made less creepy by the fact that we know it doesn't turn out to be true). In *City of Ashes*, everyone watched when "Jace [took] Clary in his arms with such force Simon... thought one or both of them might shatter" and "held her as if he wanted to crush her into himself."

Another similarity between Kevin's relationship with Leslie and Simon's relationship with Clary is that when both guys seem to "get the girl," the spark is short-lived. The only thing that's more obvious than Kevin's pining in the first half of *St. Elmo's Fire* is Leslie's lack of passion for him when they are finally together in the second half. Like Simon in the beginning of *City of Ashes*, Kevin has the only thing he's ever wanted—the girl he's secretly loved for so long. But it's a crushing revelation (Alec's infidelity) that brings Kevin and Leslie together, not genuine interest on Leslie's part, just as Simon gets a chance with Clary only after she learns that Jace is her brother.

In both cases, the girls are emotionally devastated by the realization they can't be with the guys they truly love. So whom do they turn to? The guys who love them so much they are willing to be the rebound guys. It's easy to fall back on someone you know is waiting in the wings, especially if your heart and self-esteem are in pieces at your feet. Who better to glue you back together than your best friend? Unfortunately, gluing you back together isn't usually enough to turn friendship into attraction.

Exhibit E: *The proof is always in the pudding, or in this case the kiss.*

In *City of Ashes*, Clary describes kissing Simon as "a gentle sort of pleasant, like lying in a hammock on a summer day with a book and a glass of lemonade," while kissing Jace is the opposite of pleasant, "like opening up a vein of something unknown inside her body, something hotter and sweeter and bitterer than blood." Hmm...let's see, "a book and a glass of lemonade" or "hotter and sweeter and bitterer than blood"? Which one would you choose?

It's worth noting that Leslie doesn't really choose at the end of *St. Elmo's Fire*, claiming she needs some time without Alec or Kevin to decide what's right for her, but who are the screenwriters kidding? We all know Leslie was just throwing her best friend, Kevin, a bone. In a month, you can bet she was making out with Alec again, and they probably didn't need a Seelie Queen to make it happen.

Case Study 4: The Outsiders *(Kathleen Rowell, Based on the Novel by S. E. Hinton, 1983)*

The film *The Outsiders*, based on the book by the same name, is a case study in another aspect of the Duckie effect. No matter how gorgeous and heroic the best friend is, the other guy is more gorgeous, more heroic, more mysterious—more *everything*.

In *The Outsiders*, Ponyboy, a working-class Greaser, becomes friends with Cherry, a gorgeous Soc (short for socialites, the rich kids in the novel) from the other side of the tracks, when he chases off some other Greasers harassing her at the movies. Cherry and Ponyboy end up becoming friends, and he likes her. Granted, he hasn't been pining for Cherry for years, but a crush on a Soc girl is no joke; it's something we eventually learn can get you killed.

Dallas Winston is also a Greaser, and a friend of Ponyboy's. But he doesn't spend his time reading poetry and contemplating the social divide between the Greasers and the Socs like Ponyboy does. Dallas is too busy drinking and fighting and running from the cops, when he isn't robbing liquor stores and hitting on girls. Cherry meets Dallas only once, and he's less than charming, but her takeaway from the experience says it all: "I hope I never see Dallas Winston again. If I do I'd…probably fall in love with him." Dallas embodies the bad boy, something the best friend will never be.

Exhibit F: Jace embodies the bad boy, and Clary is immediately attracted to him because of it.

In *City of Ashes*, Simon remembers the first time he noticed the way Clary reacted to "the blond boy with the strange tattoos and the angular, pretty face [Jace] as though he were one of her animated heroes come to life. [Simon] had never seen her look at anyone that way before"—including him. Jace is Clary's Dallas Winston, a gorgeous, rule-breaking bad boy, who seems more like a superhero with his tough exterior and I-don't-need-anyone attitude. From the moment she meets Jace, she can't forget him, and despite his sarcastic comments, she can't fight her attraction to him any more than Cherry can fight her attraction to Dallas. Like Simon, Ponyboy doesn't get the girl either.

Lots of readers will argue that Simon does get the girl, it's just not Clary, and that's true. But that doesn't challenge the basic principle of the Duckie effect, which is the *best friend* never gets the girl.

The Exception

It's interesting to note that the opposite outcome is true when the person in love with her best friend is a girl instead of a boy. In literature and film, the girl always seems to get the guy, even if the girl is shy, geeky, or dare I say average looking. We only need to look to one '80s film to see how this scenario plays out because it's always the same; the girl is in love with her best friend, who chases some unattainable girl until he finally gets her and realizes it was his best friend he was in love with all along.

In John Hughes' 1987 film *Some Kind of Wonderful*, Keith's best friend, Watts (a girl), is secretly in love with him. Keith has no idea, in part because he is completely fixated on Amanda Jones, a girl who is way out of his league. Watts buries her feelings and agrees to help him with an elaborate plan to win Amanda's heart, which tears Watts' heart to shreds in the process. Unbelievably, as it always seems to happen when a girl is in love with her male best friend, the boy (Keith, in this case) manages to get the fantasy girl. The difference? At the last minute, Keith suddenly realizes he's really in love with Watts and chases her down the street to give her the diamond earrings he planned to give to Amanda.

So what gives? Why do the girls end up with their best friends? Why aren't they Duckies too? The message seems to be that guys don't always know what they want—or who is right for them—until a resourceful young woman finds a way to show them. While this portrait of literary and cinematic boys in general is less than flattering, is it any less flattering than the portrait of girls who undergo some sort of chemical reaction the minute they meet an emotionally unavailable bad boy? Unless the bad boy in question isn't really bad at all (like Jace). What if these fictional girls empower a few of us who are more Watts than Amanda Jones to go after our own Jace Waylands anyway, off the screen and the page? Girls going after what they want in literature, and life, always get my vote.

Couldn't ending up with a Duckie be just as empowering? Unfortunately, most film and literature heroines will never find out, though more than a few real girls know the truth: Sometimes your best friend also happens to be the best choice.

Until then, like crop circles, UFOs, the Bermuda Triangle, and ESP, the Duckie effect is an unexplained phenomenon. Only one thing is certain: Even if he's an adorable Jewish vampire, the best friend *never* gets the girl.

Kami Garcia *is the* New York Times, USA Today, Publishers Weekly, *and international bestselling coauthor of the Beautiful Creatures novels.* Beautiful Creatures *releases in theaters in 2013 from Warner Brothers and Alcon Entertainment, starring Viola Davis, Jeremy Irons, Emma Thompson, Alice Englert, Alden Ehrenrich, and Emmy Rossum. Kami is also the author of* Unbreakable, *the first book in her solo series,* The Legion *(Little, Brown, 2013), which is currently being developed as a major motion picture. You can find out more about Kami and her books at www.kamigarcia.com or follow her on Twitter at @kamigarcia.*

I've caused a lot of consternation among fans with the Jace/ Clary sibling plotline. I know this because of the amount of AUGH and ICK that have come my way over time. But isn't that what we want from a story? For it to make our hair stand on end? For it to make us question our assumptions about what sort of love is acceptable to us, and why?

You can probably tell that I've written about this too much already, as evidenced in my language having devolved to "AUGH" and "ICK," which is why I'm so glad Kendare has swooped in with this articulate essay, rescuing me from any further embarrassment.

BROTHERLY LOVE

JACE, CLARY, AND THE FUNCTION OF TABOO

There's a reason that stories end at Happily Ever After. Happy couples are boring. Bo-ring. It's all kissy faces and "honey-bear this" and "snuggle-pie that." It's sweet, and deep, and meaningful. And it makes us want to close the book. As readers, we're drawn in by the struggle, by the drama, by the *desires* of the characters. There are few things in literature more enthralling to read than the tale of two people who yearn to be together. The great love stories tell us that to be truly engaging, couples should yearn against seemingly insurmountable obstacles. The more a couple has to overcome, the more forbidden the romance, the more we root for them. The young lovers of *Romeo and Juliet* defied a family feud and married in secret. Jack Twist and Ennis Del Mar fought against societal constraints and shame in *Brokeback Mountain*. Lancelot and Guinevere overcame the constraints of common sense and decency. In Cassandra Clare's Mortal Instruments series, Jace Wayland and Clary Fray overcome the taboo of sibling incest, and they do it without ever crossing the gross-out line.

Taboo as Titillation

> *Taboo (noun): a custom prohibiting or restricting a particular practice or forbidding association with a particular person, place, or thing*

When Jace is shown to be Clary's brother, the two have been falling in love for the better part of a book. The reader has invested in them. But the introduction of incest still should throw up a significant barrier for romantic enjoyment. It should stop us in our tracks, turn us 180 degrees, give us that slimy feeling we get when we remember that time we accidentally watched *Flowers in the Attic* on TV.

This is not the reader response it evoked. Readers wanted Jace and Clary together anyway. The question is: Why? And the answer lies in the very fact that they aren't supposed to be.

Everyone loves a good taboo. Tell a person they can't or shouldn't do something, and well, you know what happens. As many people as the taboo discourages, it seems to *en*courage that many more. Even when it's incest. If you need evidence, just Google "incest stories" and watch the hits roll in.

But what is it about taboo that makes it so appealing? Why are we so much more desperate for Jace and Clary to be together simply because they *can't* be? The simple (probably oversimple) answer is human nature. People have a tendency to want what they can't have and to want to do what people tell them they shouldn't. It's the old Pandora's Box problem. "Don't open that," someone says, and instantly, a box you might never have looked twice at becomes much more interesting. Why can't we open it? What would happen if we did? What's *in* there? It's curiosity, and the need to learn for ourselves, and before we know it, the box is wide open. Or maybe humans just have a deep-seated need for suffering and strife. The impact of taboo is complicated, and mired in layers of psychology.

When we see Jace and Clary struggling with their urge to be together despite knowing that it's "wrong" and that they shouldn't feel that way, we identify with it on a basic level. We want to know what is *in* them. We want to know what would happen if they were together. But the function of taboo when it comes to Jace and Clary's romance is more complex than just that. Every literary relationship has to have conflict. The incest taboo heightens this conflict, introducing a new dimension that wouldn't be present if the characters were grappling only with inner demons and neuroses—say, a fear of commitment or a fear of intimacy. The obstacle that Jace and Clary face is outside of themselves, something they believe they cannot change. Incest is no minor taboo. It's a genetic imperative to avoid disease and defects due to inbreeding. It's illegal in most countries and carries a hefty prison term, and rules against it have been in place in some shape or form for the entirety of recorded history. Historically, people have been executed for it. It's a real hurdle, one that can't be overcome by a heart-to-heart or a good cry.

Okay, so the incest taboo functions as an effective romantic obstacle. But really, it's not just that incest is forbidden that matters here. It's the *reason* that incest is forbidden. It comes down to the nature of love and—prepare to be titillated—the nature of sex.

Sex is like the mother sauce of taboo. So many taboos find roots in sex and manage to grow so many interesting branches. Think about it: Sex in itself is a complicated thing in our culture (and in most), twisted through with guilt and consequences as well as ideals and passion. On one hand it is held as necessary and exalted, something to be celebrated, but on the other it is introduced to us as something whispered about behind closed doors, something denied to us until we are older, wiser, and not biologically related. "You're going to do it, but not until you're older." "You can do it, but not until you're married." "You're doing it, but don't talk about it!" The limits placed on sex increase our curiosity about it tenfold! And sex wouldn't be half so appealing if this weren't the case. Filmmakers, artists, and writers have delighted in breaking down barriers of the sexually and romantically forbidden practically since the invention of film, art, and writing. If sex and love were simple, straightforward concepts, why would we care to explore them, in art or in life? They would be completely uninteresting. And so the incest taboo works to complicate and elevate Jace and Clary's relationship in this respect as well. The two dance around feelings of what should and shouldn't be, alternately standing firm against the taboo and giving in to their desires, until it seems that the pair will be doomed to yearn indefinitely. Luckily, they're granted a last-minute reprieve, but by then the taboo has already done its work, investing the reader in them completely by keeping them apart for so long.

It's worth noting that Cassandra Clare uses the incest taboo as intrigue only. There is no real transgression between Jace and Clary, since they don't engage in a (voluntary) physical relationship while thinking of each other as siblings. This doesn't mean that the taboo is less relevant; rather, it breaks the taboo down to its purest form. It's not an act, it's an idea. It's an impression of utter wrongness, an ever-present invisible barrier that attracts at the same time that it repels.

To Incest or Not to Incest? Depends on Whether You Left the Nest

But why doesn't it repel, in Jace and Clary's case, any more than it does? Speaking as a reader myself, when it seemed that Jace was Clary's brother, I blinked a moment, then thought, "So what? You're in love, and it's not like you *grew up together.* Shack up already, and what the heck, have little babies who will be superstrong Shadowhunters with an uncanny talent for the banjo." It might seem a strange reaction, and indeed it would be easy to become desensitized to the theme of sibling incest with the growing frequency that it is presented in pop culture, most notably cable television. *Dexter* and *Boardwalk Empire* both recently introduced incest plots. Showtime's *The Borgias* hints at it pretty heavily between brother Cesare and little sister Lucrezia. Perhaps we're all watching too much *Game of Thrones*, where sibling incest between Jaime and Cersei Lannister, twins who have been lovers since reaching sexual maturity, is treated largely as a love affair.

Wait, nope. That's still gross.

So why is watching Jaime Lannister make googly eyes at Cersei so much creepier than seeing Luke and Leia kiss in *The Empire Strikes Back*? The key is in the phrase "grew up together." Jace and Clary didn't. Time to introduce some science.

Sexual aversion to our siblings is often attributed to something called the Westermarck effect, which states that humans are unlikely to view individuals with whom they are raised from a young age as sexually attractive. Whatever it might be called, this knowledge is intuitive to most people. You don't lust for someone who broke your toys and vied with you for your parents' attention. Jace and Clary didn't break each other's toys. They met as young adults, as strangers. Hearing Isabelle tell Clary that Jace is "damn sexy" and then refer to him as her brother is far more disturbing than an entire book of Jace and Clary's tortured pseudo-incestuous longing, because they were raised together in the same house as siblings.

Jace and Jonathan have shared an upbringing. Both were raised by the same father, and this is why Jace feels more sibling empathy for Jonathan than for Clary. It's also why the pseudo-incest that keeps Jace and Clary apart in the first three books can serve as a romantic obstacle rather than being a creepy bucket of yuck.

The Blood Tie

Some might say that the theme of incest in the Mortal Instruments is a nonissue, since it is revealed that Jace and Clary are in fact not siblings but rather that Jace is the son of Stephen and Celine Herondale. But to this I say: Nay. For the better part of two novels—the ending of *City of Bones*, the entirety of *City of Ashes*, and a majority of *City of Glass*—the reader is led to believe that Jace and Clary share Valentine Morgenstern as a father, and this pseudo-incest becomes the main obstacle in their relationship. But is the relationship between Jace and Clary really pseudo-incest? Or is it incest-incest?

When it is discovered that Jace and Clary are in fact not siblings, the romantic in us sighs in relief. Finally! They can be together. But nearly at the same time, the reader is informed that Jace and Clary share the blood of the angel Ithuriel, injected into them undiluted by Valentine when they were still in the womb. With the idea of incest so fresh in mind, this revelation is enough to bring the taboo back to the forefront. One type of pseudo-incest is traded for another. "I gave my blood to Valentine Morgenstern, and he put it in his baby boy," says the demoness Lilith in *City of Fallen Angels*, referring to Clary's biological brother, Jonathan Morgenstern. "You might almost say that in a way, I am Jonathan's mother." By the same logic, the angel Ithuriel could claim paternity over Jace and Clary, and we're back in the incest boat. This new claim asks us to look back over the course of the previous novels; it practically begs us to examine what the blood tie means and the ways it may have influenced Jace and Clary's dynamic. "Blood calls to blood," the Queen of the Seelie Court says in *City of Fallen*

Angels. And indeed it does, within the Mortal Instruments series, and elsewhere.

The theory of genetic sexual attraction postulates that we are predisposed to find those individuals with similar genetic material particularly attractive, if this predisposition has not been suppressed by the Westermarck effect. It makes sense. The narcissist in all of us finds similarities attractive. We delight in common traits and preferences. So two siblings who don't know they're siblings may find themselves attracted to each other on a basic genetic level. Similar pheromones in an unknown sibling may trigger reactions in the brain, as can similar notes in a relation's voice. Siblings who were separated at a young age and later reunited often report strong and almost instant feelings of attraction, even euphoric crushes so extreme that it seemed impossible not to act on their urges. This is no small phenomenon; according to an article in the *Guardian*, as many as 50 percent of these reunions result in strong or obsessive feelings. Couples who break the incest taboo and become intimate insist that the intensity of their relationship trumps every other, that it is heightened by their genetic similarities and can't possibly exist outside of those similarities. Jace and Clary seem to have this level of affection and intensity. Could it be due to their shared angel blood?

From the moment Jace meets Clary, he is unable to stay away from her. It is he, not the other Shadowhunters, who identifies the Shadowhunter blood within her, almost as if he senses it. Throughout the books we (and the characters themselves) are made aware of certain similarities. Both are strong-willed and unlikely to do as they're told. Though Clary has red hair, their appearances are both described as "golden" in various degrees. And not long after their first meeting, Clary makes note of Jace's hands and that they are "slim and careful, like the hands of an artist." Much like her own hands. She also notes a subconscious similarity to her mother in one of his facial expressions, which she calls "scary-calm." This might not seem relevant, since Jace and Clary's mother aren't related, but it is often said that Clary strongly resembles her mother, making Jace's resemblance actually a resemblance of herself.

Blood's tendency to call to blood may have a lot to do with Jace and Clary's fast connection. Within the theory of genetic sexual attraction is the idea that the bond is further strengthened by a subconscious need to form a connection to the genetically similar person in a way that might have been formed during a shared childhood. On a subconscious level, the longing for the intimacy missed with this person who is so linked to you asserts itself. This is more evident in Jace than in Clary, possibly because he had an abusive childhood with no real bonds. When Jace meets Clary, although initially aloof, he quickly breaks down and tells her things about his childhood and his father that would seem out of character for such an untouchable guy, were the connection with Clary not already there, in his subconscious and in his blood.

So what? you say. So Jace and Clary are siblings in the eyes of the Angel. Aren't all Shadowhunters essentially one big inbred clan? It probably helps their case as a couple, rather than hurts it, because Shadowhunters don't breed with mundanes. They're purists, preserving the blood, and while that might seem a bit exclusive, it certainly seems to be in their best interest. Undiluted angel blood is strong. Jace and

Clary are the only two Shadowhunters to have it straight from the source, and they're the strongest Shadowhunters of their generation. There is no such thing as pseudo-angel blood incest. The idea doesn't bring up strong feelings of aversion, and there are no immediate psychological road-blocks to Jace and Clary's relationship. It should all be roses and ponies from here.

But it won't be.

The entirety of the Jace/Clary dynamic has been root-ed in the incest theme. Their blood is what called them and bonded them together; the taboo is what forced them apart. Now that the taboo is gone, count on the other blood issues between them to contribute to significant problems.

At the conclusion of *City of Fallen Angels*, the blood of Jace and Jonathan Morgenstern mixed, and Jonathan speaks inside Jace's mind. They are one, become more truly brothers. And Jonathan was the only one to truly violate the incest taboo, when he kissed Clary in *City of Glass*, posing as Sebastian Verlac but knowing full well that she was his sister. Even after his identity is revealed, many interactions between them are peppered with instances of him stand-ing creepily close or finding excuses to touch her. Within the pages of *City of Lost Souls* he goes even further, to the point of sexual assault. For the purposes of this essay, the assault isn't the issue. Rape is about power, about victimiz-ing someone, not about forming a connection. And before he committed the assault, Jonathan Morgenstern *wanted* a connection. He wanted to see similarities between him and Clary, for her to be his true sister. He says: "When I first met you, in Idris, I had hopes—I had thought you would be like me. And when you were nothing like me, I hated you. And then, when I was brought back, and Jace told me [that you killed our father and didn't care], I realized that I had been wrong. You *are* like me."

It's this sibling similarity that leads him to believe that Clary can be brought into the fold. It makes him believe that she's worthy to be part of his cause.

The incest taboo between Jonathan and Clary doesn't function in the same way as the taboo between Jace and Clary does. The reader is meant to be repulsed. But that is due more to the fact that Jonathan is a vile villain than it is to his desire to connect physically with Clary despite their shared parentage.

Blood, whether the blood of the angel that makes a Shadowhunter a Shadowhunter or the blood that ties you to your family, is important in the Mortal Instruments series. Jace and Clary's blood has brought them together, united them, and then threatened to separate them forever. It has twisted them, turned them, and defined who they are. But now we know the truth of it, and we know where they stand. Or do we?

If you've been reading the Mortal Instruments for any length of time, you know that only two things are certain: Dead doesn't necessarily mean dead, and you never know whose blood is going to wind up running through your veins.

Kendare Blake grew up in the small city of Cambridge, Minnesota. She studied finance at Ithaca College and Creative Writing at Middlesex University in London. Now she inhabits Washington State, along with her husband, Dylan, and two catsons: Tybalt and Mojo Jojo. There's also a horsedaughter, but she's all grown up now and lives on her own, obviously too busy to ever call or write. Kendare is the author of Sleepwalk Society, Anna Dressed in Blood, Girl of Nightmares, *and the upcoming* Antigoddess *trilogy.*

Friends: Where would we be without them? We'd be chasing people who are terrible for us, making unfortunate fashion choices, and watching terrible movies alone. We'd be standing at the edge of a decision, wondering what the hell we should do. We'd forget to laugh. Gwenda Bond expresses a sentiment we don't hear often enough—that friendship is its own kind of love story.

Asking for a Friend

So much of life as a teenager is spent trying to find that special person. Maybe you know the one I mean.

The person who always seems to get you, the one you can call at any time day or night for reassurance or bail money, the one you talk to for hours sharing your darkest secrets without ever worrying they'll tell, the one who always, *always* has your back no matter what idiot thing you just did. The one you have inside jokes with, and ice cream binges, and bad movie marathons. The one whose betrayal would break your heart and smash your soul into teeny-tiny pieces with the pure shock of it.

Who doesn't remember this yearning? And if you think I'm talking about love, well, you'd be wrong—at least in part. Sure, we all want to meet a gorgeous being who longs to make out with us and whom we long to make out with in return. But when I think back to my teen years, to the people I dated, it's usually with half-affectionate, half-mortified laughter. We were so young, so inept and ill-suited for each other. We were actively bad at making out. The dissection of everything that happened on a date afterward with friends was usually way more fun than the date itself.

So, no, the relationship nostalgia I'm talking about is a different kind entirely, and I'd bet I'm not alone. And this need sticks with you into adulthood, perhaps evolving, but still there (and if you're lucky, met). It's something that can be just as important as romantic love but is rarely treated that way in stories: friendship.

But the Mortal Instruments series is an exception. The phenomenon of undervaluing friendships—or at the very least taking them for granted—can sometimes be a side effect of the understandable focus many readers have on the series' great epic loves—Clary and Jace, Alec and Magnus, Isabelle and Simon (a girl can hope). But Cassandra Clare never forgets how important friendships are in her characters' lives. The novels never give short shrift to the *other* epic love stories being told too, the ones that involve old friends, new friends, and, most important of all, best friends.

Beyond the One True Pairing

The lack of attention given to just-friendship when love is also in the air has been noted before. No less than C. S.

Lewis—himself one half of a famous literary bromance with J.R.R. Tolkien—wrote in *Four Loves*, "To the Ancients, Friendship seemed the happiest and most fully human of all loves; the crown of life and the school of virtue. The modern world, in comparison, ignores it." Of course, a few paragraphs later, he also nails one of the reasons why that's so, pointing out that there's "nothing throaty about it, nothing that quickens the pulse or turns you red and pale." Romantic love is more dramatic, more edge of the seat. Hearts pound, palms sweat, cheeks burn, breath quickens. Friendship has different, subtler effects. It brings other rewards, and other costs.

I'm not disputing the importance of connections centered on romantic love, because that would be insane. Clary + Jace = forever. What I'm suggesting is that the connections of friendship in the series are just as real, strong, and important as the smooch-inclined ones. But it's also not as if those types of relationships and friendship are mutually exclusive, so some further definition is in order to make clear where friendship fits into the mix.

Acknowledging areas of overlap is important partially because the overarching story of the series, in which Team Good battles Team Evil (or, at times, Team Less Good) to protect the world, is played out primarily through relationships. The Mortal Instruments is all about the ever-evolving connections between people, whether they're human or supernatural beings. Clare explores a wide variety of relationships over the course of the series, all with their own specific depth and complexity: fathers and sons, mothers and daughters, Shadowhunters in a *parabatai* bond, siblings (including those who turn out not to be siblings after all, whew), to tick off just a few examples. Throw the bad history between

Downworlders and Shadowhunters or the natural dislike between vampires and werewolves into the mix and things get even more interesting. But since we're talking here about one specific variety of relationship—friendship—what is it that makes a friend a friend?

The answer isn't entirely straightforward. Without a doubt, friendship *can* be a facet of another type of relationship, such as a romance or a sibling bond. But it's just as telling that it *isn't* always present. We all know people whose familial relationships definitely don't come with the kind of easy closeness and unstated trust that characterizes the best friendships. The phrase "close as sisters" may be used to describe friends, but we all know sisters who aren't close at all. Can friendship be separated from a romance in the same way? Of course it can. Anyone who's ever broken up with someone only to never see or speak to them again can vouch for that. For the purposes of this essay, I'm defining friendship as a specific form of closeness that may be the sole basis of a relationship—as with Clary and Simon—or may be an additional element of a relationship—as with Alec and Jace. Friendships aren't forced into existence by bonds of blood or sexual history and chemistry. On some level, a friendship always requires a choice. And, as the Mortal Instruments clearly demonstrates, that choice can be one of the most important ones we ever make.

Notably, in *City of Bones*, the first relationship we're introduced to is one that will be among the most significant of the series. When we meet Clary and Simon heading into Pandemonium, everything about the way they are with each other signals that they have a long-established friendship. The ease with which they banter and the way they so clearly know each other's preferences (Clary informing Simon that he hates trance music) shows off their common friend short-hand. Simon immediately trusts what Clary says and goes for help when she reveals she's seen two strange boys with knives, even if he didn't see them. All of this lets us know that this isn't going to be one of those books where the pro-tagonist's so-called best friend disappears the moment the sexier members of the "other" world make an appearance. Simon is important. And Clary and Simon's friendship will be tested, as much as any other relationship in the series.

Just as Simon and Clary always describe each other as "best friend," so Jace describes Alec. In addition to having grown up together and being close friends, Jace and Alec are also *parabatai*. They fight together, and they have each other's backs, but the *parabatai* bond means more than that. *Parabatai* are described as being "closer than brothers," and, of course, they are also forbidden from falling in love with each other. In a very real sense, the *parabatai* bond is a pledge that formalizes friendship between warriors in the same way marriage does love. *Parabatai* know each other in a way no one else is able to. Alec is able to fake out everyone—even Isabelle—when Jace is imprisoned by the Inquisitor in *City of Ashes* by pretending to sell out his friend. But if they had the same bond with him that Jace does, they'd have instantly seen through his fakery, and known that his only intention is to help Jace get free. Alec doesn't flinch when Jace says Valentine asked him to join Team Evil; he knows, without a doubt, that Jace would never have agreed *and* he understands that Jace needs reassurance that Alec would never believe he would. Jace is someone who needs other people's good opinion of him, because he's so quick to turn on himself. Alec knows this, because he knows his best friend.

But what about when it isn't so clear whether a pair is meant to be or meant to be just friends? The Mortal Instruments proves more than once that the boundary between platonic friend and lover often appears more porous than it is…at least to the one who wants to make it across.

Unrequited Never Felt So Good

Both Alec and Jace's and Simon and Clary's friendships start the series with a one-sided crush destined to be crushed. Believing you are in love with your best friend is an entirely understandable thing. In real life, the best romances are either built on friendship or quickly grow to include one; otherwise it's all chemistry, no trust and camaraderie. But who hasn't been confused thinking that this person they share so much with might be able to love them in *that way* too? And is there anything worse than someone forcing the issue?

Take Simon and Clary's relationship at the beginning of *City of Bones*, before they meet the Shadowhunters. This earliest incarnation of their friendship almost seems thin and strained—but only because of how strong it later becomes. Yes, they are best friends with a history stretching back to childhood, with great knowledge of each other's quirks and with great affection for one another. But there's also a wall between them, with one side made up of Simon's desire for their relationship to become romantic and the other by Clary's obliviousness at first and then tolerance of that desire. Their friend shorthand is compromised by the fact that one side—Simon—often indicates or says something to the other—Clary—that she isn't fully reading, understanding, or seeing. Until, that is, the issue of Simon's one-sided romantic feelings for Clary is forced.

That finally comes in *City of Ashes*, when these two best friends step over the line and test the make-out waters following the revelation that Clary and Jace are brother and sister. It doesn't quite go how either expects. From the confusion that Clary feels when Simon calls her his girlfriend and it rolls off his tongue so easily, to the underwhelming emotional impact of their kissing on Clary and even how fast Simon falls asleep when she goes to change into her pajamas, we know this can only end in tears. But, instead, because this is a Cassie Clare book, it ends in blood.

When the Queen of Faerie announces that Clary must stay behind because she tasted faerie food, she also offers an out. A kiss, she says, and there's a round robin of combinations proposed—Simon steps up to kiss Clary, and she thinks about how she's not entirely comfortable with the prospect in this situation or any other, a tacit admission that the budding effort at romance isn't going to work. But when Jace and Clary engage in their thinking-of-anything-*but*-England kiss, Simon sees the truth, even if he's not ready to admit it yet either. Hurt, he takes off and gets himself killed. Or, rather, undead. One of the series' most heartbreaking moments is Simon's death scene in Clary's arms, with her last words of "Simon, I love you" and her protective lashing out against Jace when she thinks he might try to kill Simon for good. Her tender insistence that Simon be buried in a Jewish cemetery for his rising, on being there when he claws his way from the ground—those are the moments when it becomes certain that not only will their friendship survive the crash-and-lukewarm-burn attempt at romance but it will be stronger because of it.

For Simon, the realization that this romance is doomed doesn't happen quite so early. The first time he and Clary are reunited after his transition to being a vampire, he thinks about the threshold toward romance they've crossed as "fragile as a flickering candle flame," and he also believes that it will be his fault if it breaks and that "something inside him would shatter too, something that could never be fixed." The good thing is that he's wrong, and by the end of the novel, he's ready to openly acknowledge he'd rather have something real with Clary than a false love affair. He finally understands that what matters is that his and Clary's friendship survives—and it does, and he does. By *City of Fallen Angels*, he's dating Izzy and Maia at the same time, and when he and Clary end a phone conversation with simple declarations of love for each other, Simon reflects that he'd had so much trouble saying those words for so long but "[n]ow that he no longer meant them the same way, it was easy."

In fact, the scaling of that wall between them—or, more aptly, the smashing it out of the way—is what finally makes Simon and Clary's friendship absolutely unshakable. They understand each other deeply enough that Simon goes along with Clary taking the incredible risk of going with Jace and Sebastian in *City of Lost Souls*, because he knows she'll do it anyway, and this way at least he can be there for her via faerie radio receiver. Clary and Simon's love for each other is epic—once they get the pesky prospect of romance out of the way.

The series' other set of best friends—Alec and Jace—aren't as openly demonstrative as Clary and Simon (read: no making out) but face a similar obstacle. Alec believes he's in love with Jace, despite the prohibition against falling for your *parabatai*, and he has the added worry over coming out. But Jace knows Alec so well that he picks up on his friend's budding relationship with Magnus when no one else does. And, in a pure Jace fashion, he outs this fact casually in *City of Ashes*, reminding Magnus he's the only warlock they know who happens to be dating one of their friends. When Alec protests, Jace's reaction is confusion. He wants Alec to be comfortable coming clean with him about this and goes so far as to assure him it doesn't matter.

That their friendship survives Jace not getting what a big deal this admission is to Alec—in fact, questioning why it *is* a big deal, directly and cluelessly—is a testament to its strength. Unlike Clary, Jace either hasn't realized Alec's feelings for him yet or isn't comfortable speaking to them. Jace only knows an essential fact about his friend Alec that, of course, doesn't change how he feels about Alec. Painful or not, the revelation that Alec didn't ask for is the first open reassurance Alec receives that maybe he won't lose everything if he's honest with himself and the people around him. Maybe he won't lose Jace. Maybe he'll gain Magnus. By the time Alec and Jace talk about Alec's feelings openly in *City of Glass*, the fact that these two will remain friends is clear. Jace rudely attempts to push Alec away, in a pure Jace-like fashion. He dismisses Alec's crush as existing only because Jace is safe, in that he's not a viable romantic partner. But we know this won't ultimately push Alec away—not in the sense that matters most. Sure, it takes Alec time to announce his feelings for Magnus, but the *real* relationship he has with Jace, *not* the aspirational one, is his first reassurance that the people who love him will accept him as he is. His friendship with Jace is transformational: It helps him admit who he loves.

Once these key relationships are settled—and stronger—for being confirmed as best friends (only) for life, all-new connections are formed as a result among the other people in their lives. What happens when you're the best friend who doesn't exactly get along with the other people in your favorite Shadowhunter's life? Well, it seems you make friends with them, sometimes by accident.

Familiarity Breeds Odd Couples

The unique thing about the Mortal Instruments is not just that the story honors these friendships but that the characters do too. In a sea of books where characters are often friendless until they lock eyes with someone hot across a crowded room or have a token friend who disappears once the action gets going and is never thought of again, it's a refreshing change. How else to explain Jace's unflinching decision to feed Simon his blood to bring him back to life during the climactic battle of *City of Ashes*? He saves Simon even though there's no love lost between the two of them because he doesn't want Clary to experience the pain of losing her friend. And if there's one thing Jace and Simon both seem to understand about each other from the word go, it's how the other feels about Clary. Though Simon at least briefly considers them romantic rivals, in every instance that truly matters, there's a grudging acknowledgment by both that the other guy doesn't want to hurt Clary, will protect her at all costs, and has a fierce loyalty to her. Each is aware that Clary needs both of them. She needs Jace, but she needs Simon too. When Jace is missing in *City of Lost Souls*, Simon's presence allows her to sleep at night (much to Izzy's dismay—more on that in a moment).

Just as it made for the unlikely scenario of Jace saving Simon, again, Simon's friendship with Clary leads to something even more unlikely in *City of Fallen Angels*. Not long after Simon thinks to himself that the two aren't even friends, this odd couple is out shopping for tomato soup together. Over time the boys' shared care for Clary turns into a strange friendship of its own. Simon can't *not* take care of Jace when he sees the other boy hurting. Perhaps that is partly because he knows what Clary feels for Jace and what Jace feels for her in turn, but I have to believe it's also about what he and Jace have been through by this point. They might never admit it, but Simon and Jace have chosen—perhaps grudgingly—to become friends.

And it's not so odd when you think about it. They've been through battles—plural—together. And Simon's vampirism serves as an equalizer of sorts. Jace may be the gorgeous untouchable Shadowhunter, but as Simon continues becoming the hero he's meant to be, he becomes perfectly capable of retaliating against Jace's insults. That's right: Simon starts quipping back. Male friends teasing each other is a tradition as old as time (or at least middle school) itself. And if Simon and Jace can be friends, *anyone* can. I dream of a world where Downworlders and Shadowhunters snark side by side, and it looks a lot like this.

The other odd couple with memorable scenes in *City of Fallen Angels* (and elsewhere in the series) is Izzy and Clary. Knowing she can't call Jace to come to her and check out the mysterious address of the Church of Talto, Clary texts Isabelle. Just as with Jace and Simon, neither of these two will quite admit that they trust the other. Neither wants to admit they really are friends at this point, beneath their bickering. Izzy informs Clary that their "girl talk" is normal and seems strange to her only because Simon's been her only friend. Still, I have always thought that Izzy is the one among the group who most needs a friend. Family is so important to her, but unlike Simon and Clary or Jace and Alec, she doesn't have a best friend to call her own.

Surely part of what draws her to Simon is that so much of their relationship ends up being built on the roles friends usually play for each other. He makes her laugh. They talk. She's confused by her growing feelings for him but also by the way his presence comforts her. And though Isabelle's jealousy of Clary's close relationship with Simon persists, I'd be willing to wager its days are numbered. If Simon and Isabelle work out, maybe she will finally understand—in the same way Jace does—what Simon and Clary are to each other and that their bond is not a rival to her own relationship with Simon.

This spiderweb of connections is woven into new patterns in each volume of the series. The more horrors our heroes go through together, the more resilient the web becomes. Not being friends with someone whose life you've saved—more than once—is hard. Just as it's hard not to be friends with someone who's a good person at heart, once you know them in the way that's possible only after you've seen them vulnerable. Just as it's possible to engage in mutual trust only once your friendship is established enough to chance showing that vulnerability.

All Together Now

But it's not just the warm fuzzy feeling of good friends combating evil and cracking jokes together that elevates the role of friendship in the Mortal Instruments series. There is a resonance to these connections that speaks to the deepest underpinnings of what the series has to say about love and relying on the family you make. Simon says it best in *City of Glass*, talking to his best friend, Clary. He maintains that no one is born good or bad. He says, "[I]t's the way you live your life that matters. And the people you know." It's your friends.

The arc of the central and auxiliary friendships, and the resulting lines they draw between the major characters, echoes this theme. The Mortal Instruments is a story about what love can do but also, more broadly, about what our *connections* to other people can enable us to overcome. When these characters get in too deep for their own good, the reason is almost always because they're isolated from those with real feeling for them, as when Simon is turned. Or else it's because they're being controlled—as with Jace's dealings with Lilith and Sebastian—which is a twisted perversion of love, its inverse. The message seems to be that you can survive anything as long as you don't have to survive it alone.

If Clary can create a rune that binds Shadowhunters and Downworlders to draw on each other's strength, is it any wonder that the same universe allows Jace and Simon to be friends? Relationships are power in the Mortal Instruments, and friendship has a place of pride, treated as carefully and with the same respect as familial bonds and true love. This is a series about a family chosen, not just born.

And we all recognize the longing for that. For the ones who'll travel beneath the earth to the realm of scary, treacherous faeries with us, who'll make sure we're interred in the right kind of cemetery if we die, who won't care if we become a vampire or turn out to be a Shadowhunter, who could give a damn if we're straight or gay as long as we're happy. The ones who'd risk their lives for us and whom we'd gladly risk ours for in turn, again and again—even if we'd rather just watch an anime marathon and gossip.

The truth is, we love the Mortal Instruments in no small part because these characters feel like *our* friends now. Old, new, true friends. We can never wait to find out what they've been up to, and we miss them when they're gone.

Gwenda Bond writes young adult fantasy. Her debut novel, Blackwood, *was released in 2012, and will be followed by* The Woken Gods *in 2013. She is also a contributing writer for* Publishers Weekly, *and her nonfiction work has appeared in the* Washington Post, Lightspeed, *and* Strange Horizons, *among others. She has an MFA in writing from the Vermont College of Fine Arts. She lives in a hundred-year-old house in Lexington, Kentucky, with her husband, author Christopher Rowe, and their menagerie. Find her online at www.gwendabond.com.*

One of the most distinctive things about Shadowhunters are their Marks. Rachel Caine takes us on a tour of the power invested in tattoos over the course of history, and it's a fascinating trek. (Also, I will forever have an image of child-Rachel in a biker bar, which is awesome.)

(NOT) FOR ILLUSTRATION PURPOSES ONLY

When I was a kid, the thing I most wanted, the *coolest thing ever*, was a tattoo.

This is mostly because my dad had one, probably courtesy of a drunken evening on leave in the army, but hey. My dad had a tattoo, so I wanted a tattoo, and damn those societal expectations, anyway. So what if I was a girl? In the 1970s? I also craved a floor-length leather fringe vest. My mom was *not* a fan of daring fashion choices, so I lived in disappointment on that score, but the tattoo? *Right out.*

"Only sailors and—and *girls with red shoes* get tattoos!" she sputtered, when I mentioned it. (I was not absolutely sure where the red shoes fit into all this. After that, I began looking out for red shoes hoping to spot some kind of trend. Turns out she was under the mistaken impression that hookers wore red shoes. I don't know. Don't ask me.)

In any case, when you're twelve and a girl and you live in the '70s, it's unlikely that you're going to be able to follow your budding, possibly inaccurate, sense of cool and score that sweet tat (and leather vest) you think you really, really need to be yourself. So I found other ways to express my coolness. One of them was elaborate self-administered drawings in marker on my forearms, sometimes illustrating horses or spaceships. DON'T JUDGE ME, MAN. I was creative, okay? And I always washed them off before I went home, because I was really not all that rebellious. *Outwardly.*

I say all this so you can understand how deeply completed I felt when I discovered Cassandra Clare's Mortal Instruments series, because it sparked a renewed fascination for tattoos and what they meant—or *could* mean, beyond needing to be matched with a pair of sweet red stiletto pumps. (Technically, her tattoos are really *scarification*—the art of incising a design in the skin instead of just inking it on—but that's a practice similar to tattooing. We're not going to split hairs here.)

And the fact that the Shadowhunters' Marks not only were cool but also *stored power* just blew my mind.

The idea that tattoos have very real magical force goes back not just to Ray Bradbury's incredible, groundbreaking work *The Illustrated Man* (if you haven't read it, please do, it's riveting and fantastic) but to real life too. The history of tattooing—from marks to adorn, to those to heal, protect, advertise, or punish—goes back to the earliest days of humankind.

So let's start with the therapeutic use of tattoos.

The first solid example of *any* kind of tattooing—at least to date—goes back about 5,200 years, to a frozen Copper Age corpse found decorated with some simple marks likely made with cuts and powdered charcoal. The tattoos, primitive as they were, were located just where this man would have felt pain from the advanced bone degeneration that was evident when his corpse was examined. So these were *healing runes*, placed to take away the pain of arthritis—and it wasn't just done once. Our iceman had over fifty-seven separate tattoos, which meant that some doctor/ tattoo artist—or several of them—had applied these healing marks over time as the patient needed help.

You can just imagine the conversation during flu season. *Doctor! I need a skull and snake tattoo over here, stat—he's sneezing!* Okay, so Copper Age medical care might not have been quite as efficacious as a trip to the local doc in a box today, but it definitely would have been more decorative. Plus: You get to carry your medical records around with you *on your skin*!

Take that, modern medical science! ~~IN~~ ON YOUR FACE!

Very definitely, of course, all this healing stuff correlates to the use of the runes by our favorite Shadowhunters... although theirs generally *work*. (Note: If anybody can work me up a tattoo for curing migraines, I will *pay you good money*. Clary? I'm talking to you, girlfriend, since your special gift is creating new ones. I'm sure this is on your list to develop, right after the "deliver me my own personal Jace" rune that so many other readers have already been requesting.)

Egyptians also practiced the art of the needle, but, curiously, their tattoos were reserved for women... and again, the practice eventually turned out to revolve around health and safety. For years, archaeologists (mostly male, it should be noted) thought that Egyptian female mummies with tattoos were likely "dancing girls" or "concubines"—carrying over my mom's prejudice about those red shoes, eh?

Instead, upon more careful scrutiny, it turns out that those dot-and-line tattoos and the later images of the goddess Bes on women's thighs were likely there to ease pregnancy and ensure the safety of mother and child—a kind of permanent protective amulet in a society where amulets were extremely important (they were not only worn in life but also wrapped into the linen covering mummies for protection in the afterlife). If a tattoo could guarantee such security, it would be magical indeed, and well within the realm of the Mortal Instruments universe, where a rune for strength might be needed for a run-in with a demon, and one for healing could mean the difference between making it home and bleeding out in the street.

You can *bet* female Shadowhunters would use runes for the same purposes as the ancient Egyptians did those dot-and-line tattoos. After all, they go through childbirth too.

Similar tattoo position on the childbearing regions of a woman's body appears in early cultures in Peru and Chile, although Peruvians and Chileans went well beyond the practical applications, since their designs also extended up to the torso, the arms, and neck, and in some cases even onto the face. (Obviously, the ladies of Peru and Chile did not have to go into a corporate office every day. True fact: A tattoo artist friend of mine calls facial tattoos "job killers.")

Lots of other folks embraced the tattooed aesthetic for nonmedical reasons too. Sometimes it was just for the status. My mom thought tattoos were a sign of *low* class—an association that came about only after the tattooing machine

was invented around 1900 (an adaptation of an Edison machine!) and made tattooing fast and affordable for the poorer
folks. But for the ancient Scythians and Thracians, having
a well-illustrated body meant you were *somebody*—because,
let's face it, a lot of body art meant a lot of devotion and
time from a talented artist. Keeping your art on your flesh
also meant you didn't have to take your guests all the way
home to show off your latest art acquisition. Magnificently
detailed tattoos were a very public display of your wealth
and taste...and the practice wasn't restricted to men; wom-
en have been found with the same kinds of tats (normally of
mythical creatures and animals).

You can just imagine the silence at a lavish Scythian
party when some untattooed nobody shows up; no need to
ask for his invitation, is there? The rest of the guests have
their invitations to the important events preinked into their
skin. *Awkward!*

Pre-Roman Britons were also fond of the same types
of animal tattoos as the Scythians, which might have been
what led to the Romans calling them "Picti"—the painted
people. They weren't legendary for their parties; even the Romans steered clear unless they absolutely had to fight them,
because the Picti were kinda...fierce. And probably they
looked *fantastic,* if you were into heavily flashed-out bods.

In modern Western civilization, we often look to Greece
and Rome for our cultural cues, though, and those guys?
Not notable fans of body art. In their highly rigid societies,
tattoos served instead as convenient identification. Hence,
you only got a tattoo if you were initiated into a religious
sect or, more likely, were a slave, in which case you could be
easily returned to your owner should you stray. Having no
tattoos meant you were important—the absolute reversal of

the Scythians, which must have made diplomatic meetings weird for newcomers, and probably led to a few major wars just because the ambassadors didn't know whom to shake hands with.

But eventually *some* of those Romans—specifically the soldiers—came away from their encounters with other cultures intrigued by the whole notion of body art. You can't keep a cool flash down, and by about AD 250, Roman soldiers had discovered the ancient charms of plunking down coin in a foreign port and getting MATER tattooed on their arms—which was cool at least until Emperor Constantine got religion and forbade the whole practice. Probably not the slave tattooing, though, just the voluntary stuff. The only laws Constantine made about slavery had to do with Jews not owning Christian slaves. Other than that, it was likely business as usual.

In banning tattoos, Constantine was following accepted theological interpretation of a biblical restriction: "Ye shall not make any cuttings in your flesh for the dead, nor print or tattoo any marks upon you" (Leviticus 19:28). Interestingly, this kind of supports the idea of magic being an inherent part of the tattoo process…that there could be a certain power in it that was forbidden to humans (but not, it could be argued, to Shadowhunters, who have the blood of angels in them and operate by a whole different set of laws). But, just as a thought, what if the whole reason behind making tattoos anathema was not just a desire to keep a cultural separation but for real and sound reasons? What if tattoos really *could* be magical? In some of the darker corners of the internet you'll find people who still support that theory—that inking a design on your body, especially one that might have some kind of malicious intent, provides a gateway for something more sinister. Like *demons*.

I'm not saying it's so. I'm just saying you might want to reconsider that death's-head design in favor of something more... Care Bear friendly.

Even today, there's still a raging debate about what the Bible *really* says about tattoos. Some theologians say that tattoos are completely forbidden while others interpret the verse to mean that *mourning* practices that involve self-mutilation and/or tattooing are out, but fashion tats are a-okay. Me, I'll let the responsible parties duke that out while I get something from the craft service table. Mmm, donuts!

Not all tattoos were about fashion, status, or therapy; some were about *information*. Vital and secret information. Imagine if you could supply a warning about an impending Pearl Harbor attack whether you were alive or dead, simply by having it tattooed in code on your forearm? Not only did you not have to survive, you just had to make sure a recognizable body part made it out intact. Spies sometimes identified themselves to each other via their tattoos, which also served as ranks—they helped sort out which spy was in charge. Very useful things, these tats. Today in our own culture, some soldiers are following the ancient practice of having their essential info tattooed onto their bodies, just as Japanese samurai used to do so their bodies could be returned to their families. Not only that, some soldiers have taken to having their ranks tattooed on as well. I wouldn't be at all surprised if the Shadowhunters had some kind of ranking system mixed in with all those runes too. Not that Jace would ever pay the least bit of attention to them, of course.

Everything old is new again, and so's the idea of tattoos being a great spy/espionage tool. You can now get a tattoo that's visible only under UV light, and the newest fad is getting a tattoo in an ink shade that matches your skin, so the tat is visible only at certain angles. But as usual, Chinese innovation has gone beyond the call of duty and developed an "electronic tattoo," at least in theory. It's basically a temporary tattoo that can be applied to skin, but it contains circuits, sensors, wireless antennas, and power cells...and it's ultra-thin and stretchable. Put one on and you can hack into a protected system while looking like you're wearing nothing but your birthday suit. (Oh, and also? You can use it as a hospital monitoring device, a less-bulky ankle bracelet for house-arrest criminals, and even as a wearable gaming device. SCIENCE!)

Carrying on with the information theme: Ancient (and some relatively modern) sailors used to ink their resumes onto their arms by getting tattoos that represented their journeys: a full-rigged ship to show they'd gone around Cape Horn, a dragon to show they'd visited China, a turtle to show they'd crossed the equator. So if you were hiring sailors, you obviously wanted sailors with the ink to prove their worth. At least you knew they'd survived a few journeys.

If you want to go to the most extreme versions of informational tattooing, though, you have to look at the magnificent Maori tattoo culture of New Zealand. Not only was their face tattooing designed to enhance their looks to the opposite sex, but their extremely elaborate designs—known as *moko*—told the story of the wearer's life. This included their ancestry, which was important, as well as their *accomplishments*...their status as well as their abilities. Like having a resume *on your face.* Dramatic full-face tats were reserved for men, but women got in on the act with less elaborate decorations on the nose and chin. When Christian missionaries tried to discourage the practice, Maori women claimed that tattoos on mouths and chins *prevented wrinkles*. Magic! And...coming to a beauty salon near you soon. Hey, if Botox has become a popular beauty aid, why not tattoos?

Last, let's consider the Japanese. Their Yakuza tattoos are some of the most finely done, elaborate, and sinister tattoos in the world, although the Russian criminal community, which has developed a whole new iconography for body art, is certainly trying for runner-up position in this skin sweepstakes. But the history of Japanese tattooing is much more interesting for purposes of this anthology, because popular theory is that it really evolved out of . . . *fandom*. (There's a different word for it in Japan, of course.)

Basically, in the eighteenth century, many people in the city of Edo became a little bit obsessed with the folk story "Suikohden" (the main character is kind of like a Japanese Robin Hood). In imitation of the heroes featured in the story, they began to experiment with tattooing folklore designs and story characters onto their own bodies. Mind you, many of these new tattoo enthusiasts were woodblock artists. Instead of continuing with their ancient and revered craft, they seemed to all of a sudden go completely mental and think, *Hmm, carving wood is fun, but what about piercing our skin with needles and making designs? EVEN BETTER!* Yes, they were the ones responsible for developing the Japanese art of tattooing—on themselves. *Just because the story was cool.*

This is not meant to set *you* a goal, of course, even though I know you crave those sweet rune tattoos to show your devotion to the Mortal Instruments series. Because one thing about the Japanese: When they get into fandom of any kind, they go all the way. And in the case of "Suikohden," they developed it into a whole new art form: of pain.

There's still one other kind of tattooing that relates directly to the Shadowhunters' universes: Ms. Clare has said that she thought of the idea for Shadowhunters after being shown a tattoo that was supposed to grant protective powers to a warrior, and such tattoos are surprisingly widespread in many cultures.

In tribal Hawaii, for example, warriors were tattooed with the images of gods so that they carried around a "personal deity": If something evil attacked, their personal tattoo god would protect them. *Nice.* I'm totally getting a Thor tattoo now, to protect me against lightning strikes. Also, because... *Thor.*

Even today in many areas in India and Burma, inking on a kind of "venom tattoo" theoretically will protect the wearer from the bite of poisonous snakes, an everyday hazard there. I personally wouldn't test that theory unless I was absolutely forced to do so, though. And I assume people don't go out of their way to do quality control either. "Venom tattoo tester" would probably be the worst job in the world.

Over the ages, soldiers in various countries, from Australia, to Burma, to Cambodia, to Thailand, have had special types of tattoos that were said to give protection in battle or even (in the case of full-body Cambodian tattooing) to make wearers invincible to bullets. I take it back about the venom tattoo testers. They do *not* have the worst job. Who did the R&D for this tattoo? **BANG**... "Whoops, that's not it, look, he's bleeding freely. Better add another loop on that design." That job would *really* suck.

Soldiers and Shadowhunters...not much of a difference, except in the kind of foes they're fighting. The only *real* difference is that the soldiers can't draw these magical protective symbols on themselves with a stele, while the Shadowhunters can—and can choose the ones likely to be of the most use at the time rather than spending hours getting a permanent choice that may not be any actual help.

The downside for Shadowhunters is that if they *don't* have the right rune already inscribed, they may not have time or energy to get it in the heat of battle. So what seems like an advantage can also prove, just as easily, to be a weakness—especially if you lose your stele.

After discovering all of this, I'm thinking maybe about going back to my old-school habit of Magic Marker designs on my arms. All I *really* need is some kind of really *magic* marker, and I am finally living the dream. I definitely need that healing rune, for sure, just in case I trip and break my arm again. Also, I could really use the runes for learning things really fast, being super fast and strong, and...being awesome. There's a rune for being awesome, right?

There must be, because one thing I've taken away from the Mortal Instruments series is that not only does Cassandra Clare have the Awesome rune, but it must be embedded in the spines of all the books, which are impossibly great and captivating stories.

I can really only hope that somehow, impossibly, it transfers to my sweaty hands after hours of reading.

Now there's only one thing left in my Quest for Cool...

Floor-length fringed leather vest.

On it.

Rachel Caine is the author of more than thirty-five novels, including the New York Times *and internationally bestselling Morganville Vampires series in young adult, as well as the Weather Warden, Outcast Season, and Revivalist series in urban fantasy. She lives in Fort Worth, Texas, and continues to work on development of the Awesome rune, but in Magic Markers, because she is scared of needles. Find her online at www.rachelcaine.com.*

So, Malec. This relationship means many things to many people, but Sara Ryan's essay unpacks more than just Magnus and Alec; it also examines other characters in and outside of the Mortal Instruments, ways we can see ourselves reflected.

This is a subject near and dear to my heart—I strive to let my gay characters be human, be themselves, rather than a token minority that must behave perfectly. (I strive for this for all of my characters, for that matter.) No character should have to hop to and be an "example." Each has a right to his or her own missteps and personal journeys.

Additionally: Sara's analysis of Magnus' outfits in relation to geography and history is not to be missed!

The Importance of Being Malec

WINDOWS, MIRRORS, AND CASSANDRA CLARE'S QUEER CHARACTERS

With the right slant of light, every window becomes a mirror.
—Mitali Perkins

f you hang around with people whose idea of fun includes analyzing literature (and if you don't, I commend you for reading this book anyway), you'll eventually run into the concept of mirrors versus windows.

A mirror book, as you might guess, is a book where the characters have significant things in common with the reader. For instance, a white, straight, midwestern girl reading a book about white, straight, midwestern girls would be having a mirror-type reading experience. A window book provides insight into characters and places that are less familiar to the reader. For that same white, straight, midwestern girl, a book about a gay Latino boy in New York City whose dream is to become a makeup artist would be a window read. Both kinds of books are important. If you do nothing but look in a mirror when you read, your sense of the world won't be very expansive. But if you're constantly looking through windows at characters whose lives in no way resemble yours, it can make you feel alone.

If you're a queer or questioning reader, it's *way* easier to find windows than mirrors. If you're looking for young adult books with LGBT characters, good luck: According to an analysis by YA author Malinda Lo, only .2 percent of YA books published between 2000 and 2011 featured LGBT characters. Not 2 percent; *point* 2 percent.

So what do you do when you can't find mirrors?

One option is to try to create that slant of light Mitali Perkins mentions, the one that changes a window into a mirror. But how? Mary Borsellino, author of *Girl and Boy Wonders,* explains in an interview with aca-fan Professor Henry Jenkins:

> As a queer person, or a woman, or someone of
> a marginalized socioeconomic background, or a

non-Caucasian person, it's often necessary to perform a negotiated reading on a text before there's any way to identify with any character within it. Rather than being able to identify an obvious and overt avatar within the text, a viewer in such a position has to use cues and clues to find an equivalent through metaphor a lot of the time.

That negotiation can take various forms, depending on what the author gives you to work with. If you're lucky, you have what you get in Cassandra Clare's books: both cues and clues in metaphor *and* obvious avatars with whom to identify. Or to put it into the terms I've been using, you get both windows and mirrors.

Cues and Clues: The Right Slant of Light

The first time characters discuss coming out in the Mortal Instruments, it has nothing to do with revealing same-gender attraction. In *City of Ashes*, Luke Garroway, aka Lucian Greymark, benevolent werewolf and father figure to Clary Fray, has gotten hold of a pamphlet, *How to Come Out to Your Parents*. He thinks it may help Simon Lewis explain his new situation to his mom. "The pamphlet's all about telling your parents difficult truths about yourself they may not want to face."

When Clary presents the pamphlet to Simon, he "practices":

> Mom. I have something to tell you. I'm undead. Now, I know you may have some preconceived notions about the undead. I know you may not be comfortable with the idea of me being undead.

But I'm here to tell you that the undead are just
like you and me… Well, okay. Possibly more like
me than you.

Whether you're reading to find connections to queerness or
not, the scene helps to get across that Simon really has fundamentally changed. And even though the changes include
greater strength, keener senses, and heightened charisma
(along with less appealing new challenges like the gnaw-
ing need for blood, preferably human), the fact remains: It
would be really hard to tell your mom that you were a vampire. Talking points might help.

And if you *are* looking for that link—if you're reading
that section and you've come out, or you're thinking about
coming out—it's not hard to connect your experience to Simon's, to identify with him in a way that maybe you didn't
before. Or maybe you *did* identify with him before, but it
was because he was in a band, or because he liked anime,
or D&D, or because he, like you, loved Clary. By using the
analogy of coming out for Simon's situation, Clare makes
it possible for you to start seeing a version of yourself in
the book.

But if you're queer and reading about Simon, you're
still performing the kind of negotiated reading that Borsellino describes. You're thinking about the ways Simon being
a vampire is like being queer—and arguably there are some,
but it's not like there's an exact equivalency. For the queer
reader, Simon is still more of a window than a mirror.

You can find another cue and clue in Aline Penhallow, who, it turns out, kissed Jace only because she wanted
"to figure out if any guy is my type." It's not that much of
a stretch to deduce that if guys aren't, perhaps ladies are.

(And indeed, we find out in *City of Lost Souls* that they are. Or at least one lady, Helen Blackthorn, is.)

Obvious Avatars

But by the time Simon becomes a vampire and has to "come out" and by the time we meet Aline, you don't actually need to negotiate to find queer avatars, because Clare has given you Alec Lightwood, serious-minded, teenage Shadowhunter, and Magnus Bane, style-conscious, centuries-old High Warlock of Brooklyn.

You meet Alec Lightwood in the very first chapter of *City of Bones.* But all you find out about him then is that he, along with Jace and Isabelle, is hunting a demon and that Clary can see them all but Simon can't. As the narrative progresses, you see Alec through Clary's eyes, and what she notices, most notably in his interaction with Jace, leads her to ask Isabelle if Alec is gay. The way Isabelle reacts is telling. She's rattled enough to mar the eyeliner she's putting on Clary, and while she confirms Clary's guess, she also makes her promise not to tell anyone. And it's a nice bit of foreshadowing by Clare, since Clary asks it as she and Isabelle are getting ready to go to the party given by the man who eventually will become Alec's boyfriend.

Magnus Bane appears first in *City of Bones* simply as a mysterious phrase that Clary learns while she's in the Silent City, a phrase that's linked to the block on her memories. Then, shortly thereafter, his name—or half of it, anyway—appears on an invitation from "Magnus the Magnificent Warlock" that Isabelle mysteriously obtains. Then, finally, he shows up in person, but his warlock qualities are not immediately on display; he's simply the glamorous host of a loft party in Brooklyn. Clare's first description of Magnus merits quoting in full:

> The man blocking the doorway was as tall and thin as a rail, his hair a crown of dense black spikes. Clary guessed from the curve of his sleepy eyes and the gold tone of his evenly tanned skin that he was part Asian. He wore jeans and a black shirt covered with dozens of metal buckles. His eyes were crusted with a raccoon mask of charcoal glitter, his lips painted a dark shade of blue. He raked a ring-laden hand through his spiked hair and regarded them thoughtfully.

It's clear from this description that Magnus enjoys flamboyant self-presentation—spiky hair, exuberant use of makeup, jewelry, and a shirt that references both straitjackets and SM-style bondage. And this is a prolonged description, a whole paragraph, which tells you that the way Magnus dresses is likely to be particularly significant to who he is as a character. Specifically, Magnus' fashion choices strongly suggest that he's not straight and also that he's comfortable and secure in that aspect of his identity. As Shaun Cole writes in *Don We Now Our Gay Apparel: Gay Men's Dress in the Twentieth Century,* "Many gay novels or novels dealing with a gay subject have utilised descriptions of dress to form a picture of the physical appearance and also the personality of gay characters … clothing, along with adornment and demeanour, has been a primary method of identification for and of gay men."

Not all Magnus' romantic liaisons over the centuries have been with men—indeed, in *City of Lost Souls,* he describes himself as "a freewheeling bisexual"—but his self-presentation and affect in the Mortal Instruments is most often a sort of glam-camp style that places him in a gay tradition that dates back at least to the supremely suave Victorian-era writer Oscar Wilde (whose many elegant epigrams include "If I am occasionally a little over-dressed, I make up for it by being always immensely over-educated"). As scholar Shawna Lipton writes on the blog Ironing Board Collective, "Making yourself stand out rather than concealing self-perceived flaws…[is] part of a queer aesthetic. From the time of Oscar Wilde, gay style has been associated with artifice and self-creation (Wilde wore a dyed green carnation to symbolize his preference for man-made beauty)." So if standout fashion choices are part of how you claim a queer identity, Magnus can be a particularly inspiring mirror.

But maybe you can't quite pull off identifying with Magnus, who in addition to his taste for glitter, sequins, and vast quantities of hair products has the swagger and easy sophistication that comes from his eight centuries of living. Maybe when you look in the mirror, you see someone more like Alec—still living under your parents' authority and their expectations about how you should live your life, knowing you're not who they want you to be, and unsure what to do. Maybe, in fact, you've even got a crush on someone you're pretty confident isn't ever going to reciprocate those feelings, like the one Alec has on Jace.

In *City of Glass*, frustrated with Alec for using his crush as a reason to avoid Magnus, Jace says to him: "I know how you think you feel about me. You don't, though. You just like me because I'm safe. There's no risk. And then you never have to try to have a real relationship, because you can use me as an excuse." Then Jace challenges Alec to kiss him, and Alec's response is to stare at him in horror. "If you're blowing off Magnus," says Jace, "it's not because of me. It's because you're too scared to tell anyone who you really love."

The scene in *City of Glass* where Alec finally encounters Magnus again is very popular with fans. Magnus is ably fighting off Iblis demons but is imperiled. While Magnus is occupied with the demons that are within his line of sight, Alec kills the demon that's about to attack him from behind.

"Did you just—did you just save my life?" Magnus asks.

Alec's response is decidedly irrelevant to their immediate circumstances: "You never called me back. I called you so many times and you never called me back."

It's a wonderfully vulnerable moment, one that fits with Alec's age and inexperience with relationships. But he's not the only one who's vulnerable. Magnus tells him, after calling him an idiot: "I'm tired of you only wanting me around when you need something. I'm tired of watching you be in love with someone else—someone, incidentally, who will never love you back. Not the way I do."

Even with his eight centuries of experience, Magnus can't see what's obvious to Jace: Alec is in love with *him*—Magnus, not Jace.

Now that they've both revealed themselves, the reader might anticipate that it's time for at least a kiss. But no, instead there are more demons—damn those supernatural threats and their interference with an epic romance! Alec does, however, make a vow: "We live through this, and I promise I'll introduce you to my entire family."

Google "Alec Magnus 'You never called'" and you get over 80,000 results. As I said: It's a popular scene. I suspect one reason why is because of the way it connects with queer readers' own relationship experiences. Queer readers' relationship struggles might include fewer instances of demon fighting, at least in the literal sense. But the idea of having to get through a tough situation before making a public declaration of a queer relationship is, unfortunately, one that still resonates.

(N.B.: Alec's raw vulnerability in that scene is also present earlier in his and Magnus' relationship. But if you've only encountered them within the pages of the Mortal Instruments, you'd have no way of knowing. There's a scene that includes their first kiss, but Clare didn't write it for the books. It exists solely as bonus content on her website, written as a reward for fans when she reached 30,000 Twitter followers. And it's definitely rewarding: fanservice in the best sense of the word. Alec asks Magnus if he *likes* him likes him. Magnus responds, "Are we twelve now?" Somewhat later, there is kissing. If you're a fan and you haven't read the scene, go read it—Google "Kissed: Magnus and Alec's First Kiss"—and come back. I'll wait.)

Malec Is My OTP: Fan Engagement

Google further mentions of the couple—use "Alec + Magnus" or simply the affectionate fan designation "Malec"— and you'll see tens of thousands of results. Ditto for "Malec OTP." OTP, a term of art from fandom, stands for "one true pairing," meaning that Magnus and Alec are many fans' favorite couple from the series. Start browsing those results, and you'll see readers responding in multiple ways to Alec and Magnus: highlighting significant quotes suitable for framing and/or using as a desktop background, creating fanfiction, fan art, fan videos and songs, and cosplaying.

Of course, you don't have to be a marginalized reader to be a fan of Alec and Magnus or to engage in fannish activities related to their characters and relationship. Maybe you simply like relationships where one partner is more experienced or where the couple has very different senses of style and hijinx ensue, or you enjoy the way the couple teams up for maximally efficient demon dispatching.

But if you *are* queer, the fact that Alec and Magnus are part of a fictional universe as popular as Cassandra Clare's—where, based on those depressing statistics about how few YA books have been published in the last decade with LGBT characters, you might not have expected to find any queer characters—is a significant one. Their presence alone, in a series that has been translated into multiple languages, may make you especially inspired to create your own responses to them. And communities form around these acts of creation and interpretation. Become part of one, and maybe that person who posts great photos under the *effyeahmalec* username will become a new friend, boyfriend, girlfriend, or other significant person in your life.

But wanting new friends and/or action isn't the only reason to involve yourself with characters from a fictional universe. You can also use the details the author provides about the characters as a jumping-off point to learn more about—well, in Clare's books, any number of things, from anime, to Muay Thai, to Northern Renaissance painting, to the poetry of Ted Hughes and William Butler Yeats. And when an author gives you characters with whom you identify, then removes them from the narrative for long stretches, their very absence can be, paradoxically, a way for you to connect with them even more closely.

I keep saying "you," but here's where I come clean, or out, as the case may be: I identify as queer, so I'm one of those marginalized readers I've been talking about. And when I read the Mortal Instruments series, it struck me that significant portions of Magnus and Alec's relationship take place off the page. Which makes sense—after all, Magnus and Alec are part of an ensemble cast, with world-saving responsibilities that often preclude sexytimes. But I kept thinking about how little of their relationship the reader actually sees and how that, surprisingly, didn't annoy me but instead made me wonder a lot about what was going on while they were offstage. (Not like *that*. Well, maybe a little like that.)

What I wondered about the most was this, based on their vacation as described in *City of Fallen Angels*: If you were a warlock who'd had hundreds of years to travel, what would make you choose particular destinations for a trip with a new lover who's also newly out as gay?

Here's an example of the kind of interpretative strategy that can enhance the experience of a queer reader who's interested in connecting to Magnus and Alec as a couple— and, perhaps even more specifically, in connecting to Magnus' fabulous outfits.

Magnus and Alec's European Vacation (with a Bonus Stop in South Asia)

We know from the text that Magnus takes Alec to Paris, Florence, Madrid, "somewhere in India," Berlin, and Vienna For each location, we also learn what Magnus wore—or at least one outfit that he rocked, anyway.

As we know, Magnus is hundreds of years old. He's been around for any number of dramatic cultural shifts: in politics, in fashion, in the way same-gender relationships are perceived. And since I find history, queerness, and fashion equally compelling—and, of course, they're all connected—I decided to consider each of the destination/ outfit pairs as a way into what Magnus might want Alec to know about that place and what Magnus himself might have experienced on earlier, perhaps *much* earlier, visits.

Paris

In Paris, Magnus wears a striped fisherman's sweater, leather pants, and an "insane beret." Stripes have had so many different meanings in dress over the centuries that French scholar Michael Pastoureau has written an entire book about them: *The Devil's Cloth: A History of Stripes and Striped Fabric*. Pastoureau begins his book by analyzing an advertising campaign slogan: "*Cet été, osez le chic des rayures* [This summer, dare to be stylish in stripes]." He comments: "To wear stripes, to present oneself dressed in striped clothing— if we believe the slogan—is neither neutral nor natural. To do so, you must display a certain audacity, overcome different ideas of propriety, not be afraid to show off." Not a bad description of Magnus. And perhaps Magnus bought his leather pants from a shop in the Marais, a neighborhood that in 2012 is home to many gay bars, galleries, and shops, while in the sixteenth century it was frequented by the Mauvais Garçons ("bad boys")—French and Italian "adventurers" who, according to *The History of Paris*, "created great mischief" during the captivity of King Francis I. It's not difficult to picture Magnus among the adventurers. As for the beret, it's simultaneously a traditionally French article of clothing and strongly associated with both bohemian and queer communities—within which there has always been a significant overlap.

Florence

In the Boboli Gardens, Magnus wears an enormous Venetian cloak and a gondolier's hat, suggesting that he and Alec spent some time in Venice before their Florentine sojourn. Several centuries previously, Magnus might have worn a similar cloak along with a mask and a three-cornered hat to celebrate Carnival. This costume, which was worn by people of all social classes and genders, allowed its wearers to be anonymous, which in turn allowed them the opportunity to engage in activities—such as sex with someone who was married, or of the same gender, or both—that otherwise would have been condemned. Magnus' gondolier's hat could be read as an homage to the liaisons that gondoliers sometimes developed with their clients; for instance, in the late nineteenth century, the English author John Addington Symonds, who wrote one of the first essays in English in defense of homosexuality, was involved with a gondolier named Angelo Fusato.

Madrid

In front of Museo Nacional del Prado, Magnus presents himself in a sparkling matador jacket and platform boots. (And nothing else? Clare doesn't specify, although one imagines Jace would have reacted even more violently to the photo if that were the case.) Inside the museum, there are any number of now-historic works of art that Magnus might have seen when they were new or even when they were in the process of being created. But the most notable thing about Madrid as a destination—about anywhere in Spain, for that matter—is that Magnus and Alec, were they so inclined, could legally marry while they were there. Spain achieved marriage equality in 2005.

(N.B.: About that marriage: A Malec wedding, or at least the prospect thereof, is another bonus feature that you should seek out if you haven't seen it already. Clare created a short story in postcard form about Izzy's short-lived but epic adventure in wedding planning, which she shared with fans who attended her *City of Fallen Angels/Red Glove* U.S. tour with Holly Black. Google "Cassandra Clare postcard short story.")

Somewhere in India

All we know about this stop on the trip is that Magnus was wearing a sari. Maybe he and Alec watched *The Pink Mirror* while they were there. *The Pink Mirror* is the first Indian-made film to focus on transgendered characters, and the ensemble worn by the person featured most prominently on the movie poster—a richly ornamented gold sari and veil—is one that Magnus, if not Alec, would admire. The film is actually banned in India, but what good is being High Warlock of Brooklyn if you can't get your hands on illegal movies?

Berlin

This time Magnus is wearing lederhosen—leather breeches—which he could have chosen for their associations with working-class virility, for how easy they are to clean in comparison with fabric garments, for the camp connotations that Wikipedia avers they have around central Europe, or perhaps simply for the (ahem) ease of access provided by their drop-front style. While in Berlin, he and Alec might have discussed another Magnus, gay rights pioneer Dr. Magnus Hirschfeld. "In 1919, Hirschfeld founded the Institute for Sexual Science, with which he aimed to make people conscious of their sexuality and allow people to live their sexual lives as they wanted, not just according to rules that were dictated by society," says Gerrit Horbacher, the spokesperson for Berlin's Gay Museum, in an article on Berlin's gay history. Though judging from what happens later in *City of Fallen Angels* and *City of Lost Souls*, any insights Magnus wanted to convey to Alec about the value of unapologetic sexuality were not entirely absorbed.

Remember About the Windows and Mirrors? Sometimes People Want to Break Them

You might call what I did above "fansearch" (*fan* + *research*), a nonfiction companion to fanfic. Being inspired to learn more about something when it's mentioned in a book you're enjoying is certainly valuable for anyone, but I'd argue that it's especially so when there aren't many books out there that reflect your life. Investigating history through a queer lens is a way to make a link between your experiences and what others have gone through in the past. The GLBT History Museum in San Francisco has a quote from a 1979 flyer inscribed on one wall that reminds visitors of the struggles of the queer community: "Our letters were burned, our names blotted out, our books censored, our love declared unspeakable, our very existence denied."

And while I'm emphatically *not* a fan of emphasizing the challenges and difficulties that can accompany a queer identity, it's important to recognize that even today, there are a distressing number of people who are actively hostile to anyone whose sexuality and gender identity don't neatly fit their expectations. In a post about Clary and rape culture, well worth reading in full, Clare writes:

> I get hate mail about Alec and Magnus on what I would say is about a weekly basis. I keep thinking it will get boring, but no, every time I wind up shaking with rage and walking around trying to shake it off and cool down. Since there's such a pile of it, I tend to notice the same language cropping up again and again. One of the most common complaints is that I made Alec and Magnus gay "for no real point" or "for shock value" or "to make money."
>
> I always wondered what the hell that was about. Did Alec and Magnus' sexuality have to create world peace before it was okay to include it? Are gay people existing that shocking? Is anyone dumb enough to think that including gay characters in your story is going to net you the big bucks rather than what actually happens, which is that your book gets kept out of trade fairs and banned from libraries?

Characters like Alec and Magnus, whose presence within a fictional universe as popular as Clare's puts them in front of a far wider audience than many other books with LGBTQ themes, are mirrors for some and windows for others. Readers who think Clare made Magnus and Alec queer "for no real point" are themselves missing the point. The presence of queer characters helps all readers, regardless of sexuality, get to a place where we can see both ourselves and each other more clearly.

Sara Ryan is the author of the YA novels Empress of the World *(Viking, 2001, reissued 2012 with new material) and* The Rules for Hearts *(Viking, 2007) and of various comics and short stories. Most recently she is a contributor to* Welcome to Bordertown *(Random House, 2011),* Girl Meets Boy *(Chronicle, 2012), and* Chicks Dig Comics *(Mad Norwegian Press, 2012). Her first graphic novel,* Bad Houses, *with art by Carla Speed McNeil, is forthcoming from Dark Horse Comics.*

Like Scott Tracey, I love a good villain. Without a good villain, a story is pretty weak. I loved Valentine in all of his monstrous humanity, so it is without reservation that I say: Go forth, and enjoy this valentine to Valentine. We miss him, but really, it's best he stays wherever he is ...

VILLAINS, VALENTINE, AND VIRTUE

I love a villain. Before you can make me care about the heroine's quest or whether the hero will overcome adversity to get the girl, I'm already rooting for the villain. Why? Maybe it's because good villains start at the end of the journey while the heroine grows and learns as a part of hers. Good villains are always at their best/worst. They get to act right from the start; they thrive from the moment they step onto the stage.

Or maybe it's because villains are so entertaining. When you're a villain, the spotlight is always on you; every scene you're in becomes crucial just because you're in it. Villains make their own kind of fun, and that usually involves explosions. They have nefarious opportunities in bulk. When it comes to villainy, there are no rules, no limits, and certainly no expectations—the villain's only job is to create problems and force the heroes to react.

Or maybe it's just because villains have cooler wardrobes, snazzier accessories, minions—not to mention some of the best lines of dialogue. Villains can tell you the truths you don't want to hear, and make you suffer for it.

Yup, whether it's Loki in *The Avengers*, Maleficent from *Sleeping Beauty*, Irina Derevko from *Alias*, or Voldemort, I'm Team Evil and Eyeliner all the way. I don't care if they're big or small, male or female, human or something else entirely. Give me a great villain, of any shape, size, or origin, and you'll have my time and attention, and access to my wallet for years to come.

This is one of the great things about the Mortal Instruments series: It has so many different flavors of villainy. There's a whole underground world of monsters, any of whom could fulfill another series' evil quota all on their own.

There are the faeries, who seem to show up only to cause Clary trouble (and occasionally give her a good lead on the latest mystery). The Faerie Queen tricks, beguiles, and tortures at whim, hiding her cruelty in archaic forms of hospitality such as the offering of food or drink. Even the simple act of telling a truth—a faerie mandate—is twisted to serve her villainy; some truths are wicked and sharp. Then there are the vampires, who have to feed on human beings to survive. They siphon off the thing that keeps humans from death and steal it for themselves. Not to mention all the werewolves and warlocks and other Downworlders that haunt the night.

Any of these character types on their own would make a compelling villain. Downworlders are the offspring (whether literally or symbolically) of demons, most of which are mindless monsters driven to hurt and destroy. As a result, many Downworlders succumb to impulses much darker than the ones their more human counterparts even possess. In fact, a case could be made that the evil that Downworlders do is tied directly to their demonic heritage. Either their inclination to do harm is innate (as with faeries, who are born with a cold, capricious nature), or when they transition into their new life, new instincts develop that push them to do harm (as with humans turned into vampires, who must struggle against the new desires burning under their skin).

But in the Mortal Instruments series, Downworlders aren't villains, not really. Not as a group. Just because someone is turned into a vampire doesn't mean they have to be evil. Simon struggles with the change, still wanting to be the boy he was before he was bitten, and while he stumbles on his path, he still strives to be better. Luke sought to master his werewolf side in order to keep his loved ones safe, and seems to have succeeded. Magnus may possess a physical manifestation of demonic heritage (his cat eyes), long life, and the ability to do magic, but otherwise he seems as human as anyone else.

Of all the different creatures we meet during the course of the Mortal Instruments series, there's only one who proves himself to be utterly unredeemable, fantastically evil, and gloriously unhinged. And he's not a Downworlder at all; he's human.

The Life and Crimes of Valentine Morgenstern

It's probably no surprise by this point that there's a special place for Valentine Morgenstern in my heart, a place I reserve for the most deliciously evil characters. Right from the start, Valentine's role is clear. It's in his name (or at least his last name). Morgenstern means "morning star," a reference to Lucifer, who fell from heaven for his sins against God.

Valentine, raised in Idris, was an exceptional child who excelled at his Shadowhunter training and seemed poised for great things. Unfortunately for the rest of the world, these great things skewed toward the darker end of the spectrum. He is extremely attractive, intelligent, and possessed the kind of charisma that would have served him well as a politician, if not a king. Instead, Valentine became the leader of a splinter group of disaffected young Shadowhunters who believed they were superior to the Downworlders and that the Accords that kept a peace between the two was an offense. After his father's death at the hands of a werewolf, Valentine's negative views on Downworlders became even *more* extreme, and the Circle became a rebellion in truth. Valentine no longer simply wanted to discuss the superiority of Shadowhunters; he set his sights higher than that. He wanted to break the Accords.

Valentine interests me so much because he's a man of extremes. He is an idealist who wants to see evil purged from the world, but he became a revolutionary willing to do anything—evil included—to keep the Accords from being renewed. He is a zealot who wants all Downworlders destroyed, but he is also an opportunist who has no qualms against using those very same Downworlders to achieve his goals. He is a father who loves his adopted son enough to forgive him his rebellions and repeatedly extend an olive branch to him (in his own way), but he is also a monster who experimented on three children still in the womb without their mothers' knowledge or consent and without caring about the consequences.

For a man who despises all that Downworlders are, Valentine's deeds rival any of their greatest crimes with ease. He has started wars, drafted armies of demons to torture and kill fellow Shadowhunters—the same people he was claiming to try to save—and even gone up against the angels themselves, thinking that he knows better than they. Even the worst of the Downworlders tend to kill their victims quickly. They don't keep them chained up in their basements for sixteen years, torturing them for their secrets. And through all of this, Valentine still considers himself the hero of his own story.

In an attempt to bolster his army in the early days of his campaign to acquire the Mortal Instruments, Valentine created a number of Forsaken by using runes on mundanes. He knows that the mundane body cannot handle the runes, that it becomes misshapen and twisted and that the end result is a sort of mindless monster. He knows too that once a person becomes Forsaken, there is no turning him or her back. And Valentine still condemns his army to insanity and eventual death.

Vampires drink blood in order to survive. It may not be the most noble action, but they do it to survive. When Valentine murders Downworlder children, it is with much darker motive: to quench the Mortal Sword in their blood, in order to swing its alignment from angelic to demonic.

He kills to strengthen his control over the demon hordes he needs to strike out at the Clave.

All of the things he does are in service of a single endgame: to cleanse and purify the Shadowhunter race and return it to its former glory. Once Valentine summons Raziel, he plans to ask the Angel to remove the angel blood from any Shadowhunters who do not drink from Valentine's altered cup—which means that the newly human Nephilim, still covered in Marks, would instantly become Forsaken. Such was Valentine's plan for pruning what he saw as a corrupt government and population: mass murder.

Humanity: The Root of All Evil?

What makes Valentine's actions even more disturbing is the fact that Valentine is human. He's not necessarily predisposed to acts of evil the same way demons are. While I say that Valentine is human, that's not entirely true. He, like all Nephilim (and Clary and Jace more than the rest), has the blood of an angel running through his veins. If anything, that should *bolster* his humanity. But Valentine's humanity isn't, like Simon's, a counterweight to his darker impulses. It's the *source* of them.

What does it mean to be human? The word "humanity" refers to the human race as a collective whole but also to treating people with sympathy and compassion. One of the synonyms for "human"? Humane. All three words have the same root, suggesting that treating others with compassion, in a way that is humane, is a fundamental part of what it means to be human. That because we're human, we are predisposed to acts of kindness, in the same way that the

Mortal Instruments series suggests that a demonic heritage can, and sometimes does, predispose one toward more brutal behaviors.

But being human has a dark side too. When we talk about human nature, it's almost always cast in a negative light. It's an admission of our failings. "I'm only human" is what we say when we make a mistake or when we strive for something only to fail. "What can you do? It's human nature" is what we say when we, or others, don't live up to our ideals of benevolence. In short, to be human is to wrestle with two related but contrasting ideas: that our nature is inherently compassionate but that we will act without compassion often, and we must accept not only that it has happened before but also that it will happen again.

Fundamentally, then, to be human is to know what is good, to be tempted by what is evil, and to choose to strive, over and over again, for the former over the latter. If this sounds like the same struggle Simon experiences in becoming a vampire, that's not an accident. After all, Downworlders are human too; it's what makes them different from demons. They are not mindless creatures driven only to destroy. They too can choose. (And who's to say that the root of Downworlders' darkness isn't human in origin, just amplified by demon blood beyond what a normal person experiences?)

Valentine is exceptional only in that, though he like all men is born with a choice between acts of humanity and acts of destruction, he chooses destruction almost every time. He isn't an animalistic devourer trapped between worlds, hungry only for something it can shatter apart and rend between its jaws. He's a man, a cultured man. And even though he knows the pain of loss and the dangers of war, he sees violence as having more value than kindness.

What makes Valentine such a great villain, however, is not that he is a cautionary tale about following one's darker impulses. It's that he's *familiar.* Shades of Valentine echo in every history class, every time we learn about a despot's rise to power or a cult leader who sacrifices his followers rather than be swayed from his plans, because Valentine's not trying to destroy the world, bring about the end of days, increase his personal abilities, or take on the powers of a god. He's trying to change the world.

Valentine reignites a race war. He starts an *actual* war. But his motivation is a high-minded one: He's trying to change things for what he believes is the better. He's trying to preserve—and then improve upon—tradition. Shadowhunters were originally given their powers by the Angel in order to protect humanity from the demons and the Downworlders. Valentine just wants to make them purer. Stronger. He wants to make them better. And in that, Valentine's evil is the most human one of all: evil done in the service of the same ideals that are supposed to inspire us to strive for good.

This is part of why I love Valentine so much as a villain. Take away the supernatural elements, the behavioral disorders, and his "unique" views on parenting, and he's the kind of villain we see every day. He's the smooth-talking politician filling up news networks. He's the charismatic leader of an oppressive regime who has the undying loyalty of his followers. He's the parent who just can't accept that his children are not carbon copies of himself and cannot accept that they may hold different beliefs. His behavior is chilling not because we can't imagine it but because we all too easily can.

Valentine's Legacy

Valentine's ultimate fate is particularly poignant because of *how* his plan is unraveled. When Clary creates the Alliance rune at the end of *City of Glass*, she turns what Valentine holds up as the flaw in the Angel's plan—that Downworlders have gifts that the Nephilim don't—into an asset. And she does it from a place of compassion and heart. From humanity. Valentine is literally brought down by the antithesis of all he holds dear: Shadowhunters working with Downworlders, as equals, both bringing something unique and important to the table.

It's not just how Valentine is defeated that is important, it's *who* defeats him: his children, who are strong enough to do so only because of what he has made them. They have every reason to become like him—Clary through blood, Jace through upbringing—but they reject him instead. (Even the name Clary gives her new rune, Alliance, shows how far she is from her father.)

It's the humanity in Valentine that makes him so fascinating. And in the end, it is his own humanity—his need to leave a legacy, through his children—that leads to his demise.

Scott Tracey was born and raised near Cleveland, Ohio. His debut novel, Witch Eyes, *is a 2012 ALA Popular Paperback pick and one of the top ten LGBT Kindle books of 2011 at Amazon.com. His lifelong love of villains (and a serious aversion to apples) started with the Evil Queen in Snow White. You can find him on Twitter at @scott_tracey, and on his website at http://www.Scott-Tracey.com.*

In Kelly Link and Holly Black's charming essay-slash-dialogue, they deconstruct the idea of immortality in the Mortal Instruments books (the series does have the word "mortal" in the title, after all). Is it a blessing or a curse to live forever? And how are various characters changed not just by living forever, but by knowing someone who will? There are occasional interjections by me, but on the whole I tried to stay out of it and let the discussion unfold!

Immortality and Its Discontents

IN WHICH HOLLY BLACK AND KELLY LINK DISCUSS CASSANDRA CLARE'S MORTAL INSTRUMENTS

HOLLY: When we sat down to talk about this essay, it happened to be in a room where Cassandra Clare was hard at work on her next book. We thought we would just have the conversation in front of her and see if she wanted to pitch in.

KELLY: It seemed appropriate, since this is often the way that the three of us work: Everyone doing their own writing, and stopping when necessary to discuss a plot point or read what someone else is working on and make suggestions.

So. Why do young adults (and for young adults, let's go ahead and make it *all* readers) like books, like Cassandra Clare's, about immortal beings like vampires and faeries?

HOLLY: Well, I remember as a teenager being constantly told that I was going to *change*. That every time I dyed my hair blue or declared my love for a particular band or book or thing, someone (usually my mother) would say that I would regret it once I was older. And I remember thinking that it seemed to me that the way people talked about getting older, it seemed a lot like getting possessed. Immortality is stasis, but stasis doesn't always seem like a bad thing, especially if the alternative is losing some essential part of one's identity.

KELLY: So immortality is change, and it's also stasis. The best of both worlds! I guess it offers the chance to continue to be yourself, even as the world around you changes. And that seems exciting—as if you're the thing that the world revolves around. And of course, as everyone will say, young adult fiction offers the opportunity, without risk, to explore different kinds of lives and adulthood and choices. Like science fiction, it's a literature of *what-if.* And the biggest what-if of all is, *What if we didn't have to die?* One of the very first stories is the story of Gilgamesh, which is all about trying to defeat death. Every culture's first stories are about their gods, who live forever.

HOLLY: Well, living forever seems pretty sweet. As Raphael says to Simon in *City of Glass*, "You will never get sick, never die, and be strong and young forever. You will never age. What have you got to complain about?" Is there anything to complain about?

KELLY: If there wasn't anything to complain about, then there wouldn't be any story. Stasis is the enemy of plot.
　　When Raphael (vampire) says that to Simon (now a vampire too), Simon thinks: "It sounded good, but did anyone really want to be sixteen forever? It would have been one thing to be frozen forever at twenty-five, but sixteen? To always be this gangly, to never really grow into himself, his face or his body? Not to mention that, looking like this, he'd never be able to go into a bar and order a drink. Ever. For eternity."

HOLLY: Can he even drink? Like, booze? Caaaaaaassie!

CASSIE: It's never come up before. He says at one point in the books that he could drink a little bit of coffee. Eating would make him sick.

KELLY: So no booze. No barbecue, Chicken McNuggets, or cotton candy. It's a bit like keeping kosher only much, much worse. And of course, yes, blood isn't kosher.

HOLLY: But blood is legendarily delicious in literature. I mean, Simon seems super into it when he's drinking from a living person.

KELLY: I've never tried blood myself. Although I have had black pudding.

HOLLY: I am willing to concede that Simon might have concerns about immortality, but he's largely speculating about how it will go, since he's only a few weeks into his new life. He hasn't yet watched his family age and die. He hasn't yet lost lovers.

KELLY: It does affect his relationship with his family, though. Becoming a vampire—being an immortal—is taboo, even in contemporary American life. His mother locks him out. That's the first real time we get that being a vampire (being *out* as a vampire), for Simon, has a price.

HOLLY: The person we know best in the books who has experienced both the boon and burden of immortality is Magnus. And because the Infernal Devices is set more than a hundred years earlier than the Mortal Instruments, we get to see how Magnus has changed over time. Immortality isn't a burden just for him, it's a burden on the people close to him. As his relationship with Alec grows, Alec has to figure out what it means to be with someone who has lived so much before him and will live so long after he's gone.

KELLY: For the writer, an immortal character offers a chance to tell a lot of different stories, to rework the character in interesting ways. Magnus' arc as an immortal is interesting to me for two reasons. One, his love life follows a pretty classic vampire character arc: He's loved and lost and loved and lost again. But because of his apparent physical age, he's attractive to—and attracted by—young adults like Alec. Sound familiar?

Second, he's bisexual. (Oh, and he's Asian. That's a lot of intersectionality going on!) In terms of audience reaction, his sexual preferences seem much more notable than the fact that he's immortal. That's pretty new. There aren't a lot of bisexual immortals in popular fiction.

HOLLY: Would you consider Anne Rice's Lestat bisexual? He didn't really have sex with anyone, just engaged in a lot of biting.

KELLY: Well, yes, but he's not bisexually active in the books, at least not on the page, not explicitly. There's a very good reason why it's appropriate that he was played by Tom Cruise.

HOLLY: The thing that fascinates me about Magnus is that he appears to be the most human seeming of the Downworlders we meet, because he's so friendly and up on popular culture. He buys scarves at the Gap! Raphael and Camille are more menacing and seem more inhuman.

But when Magnus thinks about humanity, even as someone with a human parent and who once had a human life, he sees himself as outside of it. For example, "Magnus had always found humans more beautiful than any other creatures alive on the earth, and had often wondered why. Only a few years before dissolution, Camille had said. But it was mortality that made them what they were: the flame that blazed brighter for its flickering. Death is the mother of beauty, as the poet said. He wondered if the Angel had ever considered making his human servants, the Nephilim, immortal. But no, for all their strength, they fell as humans had always fallen in battle through all the ages of the world." These are the thoughts of a being who might look human, who might try to act human, but who is essentially other.

KELLY: We all want what we can't have. Magnus immerses himself in humanity to keep himself human. Talking about this helps me understand better why, in books, immortals—especially vampires—like to hang around with young adults. If your baseline condition is one of stasis, you might need regular jolts of chaos, change, extremes. Teenagers are to the immortal as cups of coffee are to the writer, except that the problem for writers is that they have deadlines and the problem for immortals is that they don't.

HOLLY: So teenagers are reinvigorating?

KELLY: ...

HOLLY: Well, reinvigorating to drink anyway.

KELLY: I always wanted to ask Cassie if Magnus was in-spired, at all, by Diana Wynne Jones' wizards Howl and Chrestomanci. Cassie?

CASSIE: By Howl, yes. Not so much by Chrestomanci. I always loved that scene in *Howl's Moving Castle* where Howl dyes his hair blue. I wanted to write wizards that weren't old and gray like Dumbledore. Everybody pic-tures wise, ancient, beardy wizards. I wanted to write a wizard who was young, a New York raver, a party boy.

HOLLY: It's interesting that an immortal person who ap-pears very young is much more eerie and alien seem-ing than an aged character like Gandalf living forever.

KELLY: Most cultures have myths about figures like Mag-nus, though. Fairies, gods who appear as youths to court mortals, and of course lots of scary children who aren't what they seem. The child—or the young adult—in fiction represents potentiality, for good or evil. And that's a big part of all of Cassie's books—young adults, like Clary, who discover that they are much more powerful than they thought they were and that the world is much stranger. Or else young adults who, like Simon, get changed into something they never expected to become—maybe never even knew it was possible to be. Of course, that's a big part of young adult literature, period. It's a literature of discovery and change. You, the protagonist, have to discover the world. And at the same time you have to discover what you are that you didn't know was possible. You are changed. You change the world. The literature of the fantastic enlarges all of these possibilities.

You know what I find really interesting? Not that there are immortals in Cassie's books, but that, given the possibility of immortality, her Shadowhunters are so very, very mortal. The blood of the angel Raziel gifts Shadowhunters with many things but not immortality. In fact, as Will Herondale says in *Clockwork Angel*, "It's not a long life, killing demons. One tends to die young, and then they burn your body."

HOLLY: So that the risk of dying young, being a Shadowhunter, being mortal, gets associated with divinity, with the way that things should be. And on the other hand, immortality is linked to the infernal. Only Downworlders get that gift—warlocks, faeries, and vampires—so it must be a by-product of their demon blood. Werewolves are the only Downworlders to miss out on the immortality boat. So doesn't that imply that immortality is tainted in some way, more burden than boon?

KELLY: Well, it's always seemed to me that werewolves are the most like us: the most human of monsters. They're inside us; you're always a vampire, whereas you become a werewolf once a month. And they're messy in a way that humans are messy: creatures of appetite, who suffer and die like us.

But yes, immortality comes with several pages of fine print. You stay the same, and everything else changes. Maybe it changes so much that there's no place for you any longer, no place that you recognize or that recognizes you. Or, more important, no *one*. We haven't really talked about how immortality works in Cassie's romances, that tension between the immortal and his or her mortal lover.

HOLLY: Love is, traditionally, forever and ever. That's what we say to one another, what we promise—*forever*. It's a romantic ideal, but love would be way different if forever really meant forever. Can two people stand each other for that long? Can one person really have a single love that means more than any other over the stretch of decades and centuries? Is that a crazy way to think about love?

KELLY: Cassie's books are, in large part, about people who find real love. True love. But every love story is a tragedy, even when you add immortals. Either you're immortal and your lover isn't. (Woe.) Or you're both immortals, and after the first forty or fifty or five hundred years, the bloom is off the immortal rose. (More woe.) The immortals in Cassie's books don't fare well together.

HOLLY: We really see that with Magnus and Camille. She says to Magnus in *Clockwork Prince*, "You expect me to have the morals of some mundane when I am not human, and neither are you." She believes that love between immortals should be fundamentally different—

that rules about fidelity, for example, shouldn't apply. On the other hand, I have always thought that there was something about Camille that seemed more essentially human than Magnus. She's petty in a way that he isn't—jealous of his having Alec in exactly the way she criticized him for being jealous a hundred years earlier—and she has a way of showing off that seems to be about impressing just the sort of people she claims not to care about.

KELLY: Apparently immortality is no cure for hypocrisy or insecurity. Or humanity. So maybe that's how Camille manages her immortality. Magnus manages his immortality by flooding himself with new experiences and interests, by creating makeshift, mixed human and supernatural familial groups for himself in each new place and time. And yet he also seems to stay above it all. Camille, on the other hand, keeps herself occupied by manipulating power dynamics and personal status. How other people see her tells her what she is.

HOLLY: Yeah, sometimes I feel as though Magnus wants to be human, when he can't help seeing humanity from a great distance, and Camille wants to be inhuman, but she doesn't have his perspective. She's down in the mess of life with the rest of us.

KELLY: Cassie, do you think of Magnus as a kind of author's stand-in in the books? For saying what you want to say to your characters, about love and immortality?

CASSIE: Yes. Usually. Everything he says about burning a lot more brightly if you're mortal, I think that's true. He gives good advice.

KELLY: Do you think of him as the linchpin for the series? I mean, he's there in all of the books.

CASSIE: Not the linchpin, no. I think he could die. Like Dumbledore.

KELLY: I guess that's why the series is called the *Mortal* Instruments and not the Immortal Instruments.

HOLLY: One of the things that we sometimes forget about immortality is that it's not invulnerability. Death can come to all the immortals in the world of the Mortal Instruments.

KELLY: Well, there's an argument to be made that all forms of magic—including immortality—stand in as metaphors for money. Magic, in fantasy, often works the way that money does. Magic buys you things: long life, cool stuff, access to the kinds of worlds that people without magic can't get into. But the one thing neither money nor magic can buy is freedom from death.

HOLLY: This is making me think, as a highly practical matter, how once you become immortal, you'd be well served to spend a couple of years doing nothing but working and amassing cash so that you could live off the interest forever. Because your retirement problems are really different from most people's. Those charts that tell you how much to put away per year are not going to work for you.

KELLY: Readers of this essay, take note: If you plan to live forever, make good investments. It's like being a time traveler, where you want to make sure you've done your research, memorized some lottery numbers and the names of really spectacular stocks when you go back.

HOLLY: I do wonder where Camille's money comes from. I mean, Magnus works. He's the High Warlock of Brooklyn. As long as Downworlders and Shadowhunters have magical problems, he's got a job. Cassie, where did Camille get her money from?

CASSIE: I've decided that she had a string of lovers who bestowed many jewels on her because she is so bee-yoo-tiful.

HOLLY: Really?

CASSIE: No. I figure many vampires have money from being around so long and whatnot. Remember there's that part in *Clockwork Prince* where they talk about vampires leaving their money to themselves, masquerading as their own heirs? And they have big investments that pay out over time.

KELLY: And traditionally, vampires are good at getting more than blood from their prey. They can hypnotize their victims into signing over their estates, etc.

HOLLY: Like a sweetheart scam, but with blood.

KELLY: We haven't talked about the Seelie Queen yet. Cassie, when you wrote the Seelie Queen, what sources were you drawing on? Which Faerie Queens were inspirations?

CASSIE [points to Holly Black]: Hers.

HOLLY: Ha! The thing I find interesting about faeries in general is that they were never human and that they are essentially other. The shorthand for that in Celtic folktales is "they laugh at funerals and cry at weddings," but it alludes to the whole separate moral system faeries operate under. And in the Mortal Instruments, the Seelie Queen is not just untouched by her immortality but untroubled by it. For her, mortality seems skeevy. It grosses her out, the way you'd be grossed out by a rotting peach on your desk.

KELLY: I can see why you're Cassie's source. That's good stuff. And of course, the Seelie Queen and her court, in the Mortal Instruments, are weirdly sideways to the rest of the Downworlders.

HOLLY: Awww, that's nice of you to say. And I agree about the faeries being sideways. They've never been human. They're separate from the realm of demons and angels. They may have originated there, but now they are a people apart, self-contained and (change-lings aside) self-reproducing. All other Downworlders continue to have to truck with humanity to survive. Vampires make more vampires by turning humans. Werewolves probably can breed more werewolves but mostly seem to make more through infection. And as far as we know, warlocks can't reproduce at all.

KELLY: Humans and faeries, in fact, appear to be some-what allergic to each other. Like you said, when the Seelie Queen looks at Jace and the other Shadowhunt-ers, she sees not young men in their prime but their decay and their deaths. She doesn't get it. She says, "You are mortal; you age; you die…If that is not hell, pray tell me, what is?"

HOLLY: Well, forever for her isn't something to hope for or dread or dream about. It's a given.

KELLY: I'm guessing that complicates her love life as well. In some way that we mortals probably can't quite comprehend. Whatever it is, I'm guessing it works for her. (I keep coming back to how immortality and love intersect.) Cassie, what do you think?

CASSIE: I think there is a difference in the books between the characters who are born immortal and the ones who are born human and who become immortal. The ones who have it thrust upon them think, "I don't know how I feel about this. Everyone I love will die." Whereas the Fairie Queen has always been immortal. Everyone she loves is immortal.

KELLY: I guess the thing I want to bring up about love and immortality is that in the Mortal Instruments, they function in similar ways. The characters we care about don't choose immortality any more than they choose who to fall in love with. Love and immortality are both things that *happen* to you, at least if you start out human. And that's straight out of the classic young adult and children's fiction tradition. Think of *Tuck Everlasting* by Natalie Babbitt. Jesse and his family don't choose immortality, and at the point where Winnie is old enough to make a decision for herself, the opportunity for choice is gone. Or a story like Ray Bradbury's "The Homecoming," in which our viewpoint character is a mortal boy born to a family of immortals. He can't choose either. I can think of a few characters in young adult fiction who pursue immortality, like Bella in the Twilight series, but even Bella, in that final moment, doesn't actively choose immortality. Edward, out of necessity, chooses it for her. Young adult fiction is all about agency: the protagonists coming into the world and taking on active roles. And yet when it comes to immortality, it's extremely rare to see protagonists take it for themselves. It's usually either forced on them, or else it turns out to have been their birthright all along.

HOLLY: I wonder if immortality is often thrust upon characters (or found to be their birthright) because there is nothing particularly surprising about choosing to live forever. That's something we'd all be mightily tempted by, and I would guess it would be the rare individual who wouldn't give in to that temptation.

KELLY: I have one more thought. Isn't it every author's dream to have characters (and books) that live forever?

HOLLY: Well, authors are notoriously of the devil's party, whether they know it or not. Wasn't that what what's-his-face said about Milton? That printmaker dude. Blake!

KELLY: If the devil was an agent, everybody would want to sign up with him.

HOLLY: Relatedly, I do think that we as readers are often in sympathy with Downworlders and maybe feel more kin to them than the Shadowhunters. Downworlders seem to have lives lived less to extremes. They don't have a great and holy purpose in the way that Shadowhunters do. They seem to have big parties and stay up late and watch television. Well, possibly that's mostly Magnus.

KELLY: That does sound like most teenagers and also most writers that I know. Or maybe just most people. Maybe it's rarer to find someone who, like a Shadowhunter, has a sense that their life may be short but knows what they want (and need) to do with it.

HOLLY: That's a kind of certainty that it seems to me that many of us envy. But immortality makes certainty of purpose impossible. Immortals live so many lives that no one purpose will stretch to fit all of them. And though we've discussed some of the drawbacks of immortality, those of us left with but a single lifetime stretching before us must admit that no disadvantage could discourage us from wanting to live forever. And since we can't have that, at least we can comfort ourselves knowing that of all the things Shadowhunters fight, they are no more able to defeat death than Gilgamesh...or us.

Thus ended our conversation, as we all sat silent in contemplation of exactly which investments would be our best bet for long-term financial security if Holly was wrong and we all became vampires.

Kelly Link is the award-winning author of three collections, most recently Pretty Monsters *(Viking). With Gavin J. Grant, she coedited the anthology* Steampunk! *(Candlewick) as well as the forthcoming* Monstrous Affections. *Together they run Small Beer Press and put out the zine* Lady Churchill's Rosebud Wristlet. *Her website is www.kellylink.net.*

Holly Black is the author of bestselling contemporary fantasy books for kids and teens. Some of her titles include the Spiderwick Chronicles (with Tony DiTerlizzi), the Modern Faerie Tale series, the Good Neighbors graphic novel trilogy (with Ted Naifeh), the Curse Workers series, and her new vampire novel, The Coldest Girl in Coldtown. She has been a finalist for the Mythopoeic Award, a finalist for an Eisner Award, and the recipient of the Andre Norton Award. She currently lives in New England with her husband, Theo, in a house with a secret door.

As you will see below, Sarah Rees Brennan has a very active imagination, which happens to writers sometimes. She also has some very, er, unique opinions on what's going on in my books. But her heart is absolutely in the right place.

What Does That Deviant Wench Think She's Doing? Or, Shadowhunters Gone Wild

THE DIRTY SIDE OF DEMON HUNTING

"So, technically, even though Jace isn't actually related to you, you have kissed your brother."
—Simon Lewis in *City of Glass*, telling it like it is

I hope, with this saucy title, that everyone has flipped right from the table of contents to this essay. Hi, guys! Almost every other essay will be more coherent and intelligent than this one, but if you want dirty jokes, you have come to the right place. Welcome to Sarah's School of Deviant Literary Analysis, where everyone gets to canoodle, including Magnus Bane's magnificent self.

And since I invoked Magnus Bane's name because I was shamelessly cribbing off a phrase he used in *City of Bones* (nobody canoodles in his bedroom but his magnificent self), let's begin my list of shameless debauchees (otherwise known as Cassandra Clare's cast of characters) with a look at Magnus: warlock, Downworlder, fashion icon. Though the angel Raziel says that Downworlders have souls, warlocks are looked down on by the Shadowhunters. They would probably be looked down on by most people: It's a shady enough thing to have a parent from Hell and to know that you are born via a nonconsensual demonic arrangement. Magnus' mother was violated, and his birth had far-reaching tragic consequences, resulting in the deaths of most of his human family; no wonder Magnus does not want to talk about his father. In lesser books, Magnus might be a villain: doomed and damned by descent, by his sexual preferences, by who he is.

But Magnus is one of the good guys. He is the only character to appear in all of the six Mortal Instruments and three Infernal Devices books. (I know they're not all out yet, but trust me, he's in 'em.) Indeed, in the Infernal Devices books, there is another demon's child: Tessa, our adorable book-loving heroine, is a warlock too. The presence and prominence of Magnus Bane, a bisexual, flamboyant, part-Asian, part-demon character, in the Mortal Instruments novels says: You can be very different, genuinely and obviously different. You can love as you will and have whatever kind of fun you like. You can be banned from Peru because of that shocking thing you did involving a llama, and you still can be one of the kindest, most decent and dependable people in the world.

Magnus in the Infernal Devices helps one of our heroes, Will Herondale, for no reason other than that Will needs help. Magnus is shown as hurt by a lady he loves, and in the Mortal Instruments, he is shown as entering into a committed relationship with a dude he loves and who loves him back. Said dude, Alec, takes a while to love Magnus back, so almost from the start we see Magnus as pining and rejected as well as deeply snarky...we empathize with his longing just as we do with Clary and Jace's longing for each other.

Speaking of Clary and Jace's love for each other: It is forbidden. Nay, it is taboo. No, I mean, they think they're brother and sister for several books, and yet they can't quite stamp out the feelings they had for each other before this dreadful discovery. Their Facebook relationship statuses say "IT'S COMPLICATED!!!!!!"

Fortunately, Jace and Clary turn out not to be related. (I mean, if you buy Valentine's story and don't think to yourself: Hey, so this hot devoted-to-Valentine young lassie Celine Herondale [Jace's mom] was in an unhappy marriage and lived next door, and Valentine was also having marital difficulties ["You never take out the trash and you always put demons in our son!"] and then Celine got pregnant and Valentine adopted her kid as his own—sure, okay, normal behavior, that Valentine, he's a giver—and he *could have* popped the Herondale scar on the baby real quick so nobody asked any awkward follow-up questions in the future. That's a personal theory. Nobody tell Jace and Clary: They might get upset. I may have already told Cassandra Clare, who said, and I quote, "You're sick, dude," and, "There's something very wrong with you." So I cannot call this theory author-approved.) This does not change the fact that Jace and Clary believed they were in the wrong and could not help feeling what they felt anyway.

Cassandra Clare is on record as saying she was inspired by the real-life story of a couple who were going to get married and found out they were brother and sister. (Most awkward "actually don't save the date" notes ever, am I right?) I can completely see why she was inspired. It is a horrible thing to happen to two innocent people in love, and books are all about horrible things happening to people. So you become involved with someone, you find out something terrible, you can't entirely crush your feelings: That is a tragedy. That is nobody's fault. Human beings are complicated.

And if you give in to your mutual (*mutual* is important, kids) desires and act on them, that's okay, even if in the last analysis you decide pursuing the relationship is a bad idea. Clary and Jace never decide to date even though they're related because holy complications, Batman. They do, however, make out wildly twice. Admittedly, once when Jace is in a fit of self-loathing, and one time the Queen of the Faeries makes them do it.

FAERIE QUEEN: Faerie Queen says kiss. Basically, being Queen of the Faeries is 70 percent voyeurism, 30 percent crafting giant flowers to wear on my head.

JACE AND CLARY: We're related.

FAERIE QUEEN: I know! I love me some *Flowers in the Attic* shizz.

Just because they enjoyed it doesn't mean you didn't violate them, Faerie Queen! And they're not bad people for enjoying it, or for feeling the way they do. The reader sympathizes with them.

Speaking of reader sympathy, I once read a review of one of Cassandra Clare's books online that said that her talent would trick you into believing Magnus and Alec's relationship was beautiful instead of wrong. I found that sad, of course, because it is sad that in this day and age there are people, genuinely good and well-meaning people, who think that (a) love is wrong and (b) what consenting adults get up to is any of their business. I found it inspiring too, though—if even people who think like that found the relationship beautiful, perhaps it dropped a seed of tolerance and love there. And for those who didn't start from the place of "This is wrong, terrible and wrong!" but who started from a place of being undecided or ignorant or oblivious...well, maybe Magnus and Alec's relationship made them aware and accepting. In the words of noted philosopher Lily Allen, "Look inside your tiny mind/and look a bit harder." These books encourage everyone to do that, simply by presenting a world that has all kinds of people in it. Presenting such a world is a risk, of course: Many readers, like the reviewer mentioned above, find a diverse world perverse in some way. But that diversity is also something that makes the world of the books richer, the books themselves better, and the minds of those reading them broader.

Which might just be a long way of me saying, "Rock on with your bad selves, you deviants." And speaking of deviants...

Not many gorgeous young heroes of YA novels share a kiss with warlock dudes, unless their wanting to share a kiss with dudes is the entire premise of the novel. Will Herondale of the Infernal Devices got snogged by Magnus Bane and then wandered off in a slightly drugged-up haze. It was not the most scandalous thing that had ever happened to Will. It was not even the most scandalous thing that happened to Will *that day*.

Jace Wayland-Morgenstern-Herondale-Lightwood (Jace has three daddies, okay, and they're all varying degrees of evil) is like Will in that this is a dude who's probably straight but open to new experiences. It's not all running around naked with antlers on his head and adopting the alias Hotschaft von Hugenstein: Jace also offers to kiss Alec to address the question of Alec's attraction to him, and does make out with Aline Penhallow on request to ascertain her orientation. I wonder how that conversation went.

ALINE: Yo, Wayland-Herondale-Morgenstern-Lightwood! That's a mouthful.

JACE: That's what all the ladies tell me.

ALINE: Good straight-to-the-filthtastic point! I hear you're foxier than the Fantastic Mr. Fox.

JACE: And the rumors are true!

ALINE: I don't see it myself.

JACE: Maybe if I turned to the side? I've been told my profile is allu—

ALINE: No. I've also been told you're quite the Casanova.

JACE: Well, not to brag, but I've nova'd a few casas in my time.

ALINE: Excellent. So you feel you could arouse a lady, if a lady was capable of being aroused by a dude.

JACE: Oh. Ohhhh. Oh I understand, I have an adopted brother who's...

ALINE: Do something more useful with your mouth than talking, I feel like I'm getting gayer by the second.

JACE: Challenge accepted!...

ALINE: Thanks, man. You have confirmed for me beyond a shadow of a doubt that I am super, super gay. I cannot describe to you how intensely I am not attracted to you.

JACE: ...Thanks. But objectively, I'm totally an eight, right?

ALINE: Later, dude.

JACE: Seven and a half?

ALINE: Awkward when your sister walked in. Well, could've been worse, it could have been a girlfriend of yours.

JACE: Ahahahahahahahaahahahahahahahahahahah ahahahahahaha!

ALINE: ...I'm going to leave you to laugh hollowly and psychotically on your own.

JACE: Good luck with your complicated love life.

ALINE: Same, dude. Same.

Oh, Jace Herondale-Wayland-Lightwood-Morgenstern, Shadowhunter by day, Shadowhunters' sex therapist by night. Our hero, ladies and gentlemen.

It's not like we're lacking perversion in other relationships. There's also Simon and Maia, who date even though he's a vampire and she's a werewolf and they are destined enemies, and Simon and Isabelle, the vampire and the Shadowhunter (shark and shark hunter is coming, I know it!).

Demons, Shadowhunters, vampires, and werewolves are not real. (AUDIENCE: Glad you've cleared that up for us, Sarah. This is such an insightful essay!) No, really, but listen, this is important, because supernatural creatures have

often been used as analogies for those seen as the Other—people of color, people with religious beliefs different from Christian, people who aren't heterosexual—because it was seen as taboo to actually represent them. It is not taboo anymore—or at least it shouldn't be—and this means that supernatural analogies for representation and actual representation exist in the same books, often in an overlapping way. Maia is half African American and a werewolf, Magnus is half Asian and a warlock, Jem is half Chinese and a Shadowhunter, Simon is Jewish and a vampire.

I like the supernatural as analogy fine—for instance, I love when Simon is trying to come out as a vampire using the language of coming out from a gay pamphlet—but analogies work only up to a point. Having a supernatural character "come out" isn't actually the same as a character coming out as gay, and can't be treated entirely as if it is. Simon shows this is an imperfect analogy by how he adapts the language. He cannot leave it as is because that won't work. "The undead are just like you and me…Possibly more like me than you" (*City of Ashes*). The lust of a vampire for blood and a person for sex are ultimately different, and that has to be clear. Being a person of color and being gay are different things, though, again, they can overlap—in Aline's case, for instance—and that has to be clear. Fancying people of both sexes and fancying your sibling, also two very different situations! Hella not the same.

There are, however, commonalities. Stretching over both the supernatural and the real in these books is the issue of desire as a forbidden thing. There are rules of desire in this imaginary world: Werewolves are not meant to feel desire for vampires, and Shadowhunters are not meant to feel desire for Downworlders. Also accurately represented,

however, is the attitude of some to desire in the real world. Tessa in the Infernal Devices worries that she shouldn't be feeling hot in the pantalettes for a guy—let alone, oh horrors, somebody pass me the smelling salts—TWO guys. Some think women should not feel desire at all, or if they do should feel it toward One Man to Rule Their Lady Parts Alone. Some think women should feel no impulses toward violence. Some think that people should not feel desire for people of the same sex, and Shadowhunters actually have a hidebound attitude about that. Some think people should not feel anything more than desire—should not feel love—for those of a different social class or a different race.

We see all of that in Cassandra Clare's books. By showing us a myriad of different desires and by showing the people who have them as, in most cases, good and heroic people, these books let people who have desires condemned by others know they can and should be part of stories. They let those who have conventional desires put themselves mentally into the position of characters who do not. We have Magnus "Freewheeling Bisexual" Bane, and we also have Isabelle "Nothing Less Than Seven Inches, That's My Motto" Lightwood, an expert fighter who has been around the block and underneath the kitchen table, baby, who loves boys and loves pink and loves weaponry. She is no less heroic than any of the male Shadowhunters: She is never shamed for her desires. She is not elevated above all other women as the sole badass babe, though: Clary is not a trained fighter, but she brings other skills to the table. Clary, Isabelle, and Maia are all shown as having different strengths and growing slowly closer because of them. And Clary, Isabelle, and Maia all have sexy desires that they sometimes act on and sometimes do not, and either way, it's okay.

The message of all these different portrayals of all these different desires is that we cannot control our desires and that no desire is inherently bad. Some desires should not be *acted* on (my desire to murder everyone I see before noon, I definitely have to get a lid on. I'm going through postmen like nobody's business), but nobody should be condemned for what they feel. And if the people involved are both enjoying themselves and want to act on those feelings...that's fine too. Take Isabelle and Simon's first time at the all-you-can-bite buffet:

ISABELLE: You should bite me.

SIMON: Well, I never.

ISABELLE: It's cool, bro, I'm consenting, and consent is sexy!

SIMON: But surely I should not treat my lady friend as a handy snack! You are not string cheese! You are not a fruit cup! You are not a macrobiotic yogurt drink!...Sorry, I miss human food sometimes.

ISABELLE: No, you should totally bite me. The conflation between the vampire bite and sex is totally a literary archetype. ˎ

SIMON: But I never fanged a girl before. I mean, I fanged Jace that one time, but I was all dizzy and we were on a boat—you know how wild those cruises can get—and it meant nothing and he was honestly more into it than I was.

ISABELLE: I believe it. Noted pervert, our Jace. Now fang my brains out.

I swear, my hand to God and Girl Scouts, that the events I have just related actually occur in the book, just as written (Isabelle-fanging in *City of Lost Souls* and Jace-fanging in

City of Ashes, to be specific and precise about my fanging).
I admit that the dialogue is pretty much 100 percent Sarah-
produced made-up. I couldn't resist: I love a make-out scene.

I will segue from talking about making out (only briefly, I swear) to talk about family. (Family who aren't making
out, guys; come on, work with me here.) The Mortal Instruments and Infernal Devices series abound with examples
of nontraditional family units. Jace was adopted at the age
of twelve, and there are strains from both sides—fear that
Jace's allegiance belongs to his birth parent, parental fear
from Maryse Lightwood that her sins or the birth parent's
sin will taint Jace. But Maryse loves him, and sings him the
song she sang the children she gave birth to, because he's
hers. Charlotte, much too young to be a mother, is nevertheless placed in loco parentis to Will and Jem: While it's not
motherhood, it's guardianship, and there's love and respect
there on all sides. Mortmain, the villain of the Infernal Devices, clearly adored his adoptive warlock parents. Even
Valentine, the chief villain of the first Mortal Instruments
trilogy, whom we find out in *City of Glass* adopted Jace (OR
DID HE? Sorry, no, he did, go on), genuinely loves his son:

> VALENTINE: My boy. My sweet boy. I could not love
> thee, dear, so much did I not love megalomania-
> cally taking over the world more.
> JACE: I'm going to be in therapy forever.
> VALENTINE: I stab you to death now. With a heart full
> of love! Know this: I would still totally stab you
> if you were biologically mine. It makes no differ-
> ence to me: I am devoted to you, and immensely
> crazypants.
> JACE: Call a doctor and a psychiatrist…
> VALENTINE: Stab, stab, XOXOXO, Daddy.

This is borne out again by the fact Valentine does not love Clary, who actually is biologically his daughter. He blames her for her mother leaving, which, putting aside the surface crazed-demon-hunter-on-mission-to-take-over-world issue, is relatable again: the parent who resents a child for taking up the other parent's attention and affection. In return, Clary doesn't love him: In fact, she murders him for being a big boyfriend-killing world-take-overing speciesist jerk. He's not her father in any real sense: Luke Garroway the werewolf is her father, if anyone is. And it is Luke who says perhaps the truest and most important thing in the books, making explicit their message, in *City of Fallen Angels*: "Be what you are. No one who really loves you will stop."

Love is acceptance, and treating people right. Sebastian, Clary's bio brother (whom she totally also makes out with, and who is also a bit demonish, and whose real name is Jonathan but I'm sticking with Sebastian because my motto is once you murdered someone and assumed their identity, murderous finders' keepers!), is actually related to Clary and Valentine, and in the Infernal Devices, Tessa and Nathaniel are somewhat related, and Benedict Lightwood is definitely Gabriel and Gideon's father. Doesn't really work out well! Sebastian, Valentine, and Benedict are bad people. (Except that Sebastian is my baby demon honey lamb, but that's not what this essay is about, however: Don't blame the demon-blood-infested player, hate the demon-blood-infesting game.) Simon is blood related to both his mother and his sister, but his mother rejects him in *City of Fallen Angels* and his sister accepts his vampirosity in *City of Lost Souls*. Embracing people for who they are is the key.

The portrayal of all these untraditional families and strange friendships conveys this: Blood doesn't matter.

Tradition doesn't matter, and following the accustomed forms and rules of family doesn't matter. *Love* is what matters. Love is the song you hear even while you sleep, and you know you are healed, and safe, and where you belong.

So what does all this talk about love and desire and strangeness really mean, in the larger scheme of things rather than in the personal-opinions arena? (Example of a possible personal opinion: "I Read This Book of Essays and I Really Think Sarah Rees Brennan Is a Demented Sex Fiend.") I'm not saying: These books are a lot about desire, keep them away from children! I'm saying: These books are a lot about desire in all its forms and about not condemning it, and I think that's valuable for teenagers—for everyone.

Let's examine what Cassandra Clare has actually done, through this addressing of love and desire. She's written one of the very few (I count two[1]) young adult books with an Asian character important enough—Jem Carstairs, via being one of the romantic leads—to get his own cover, to hit the bestseller list (*Clockwork Prince*). She has written what I would say is *the* most popular gay relationship in the whole YA fiction realm. And is popularity important? Yes, yes it is. A book is more likely to be popular if it's heteronormative; it means there are fewer obstacles in the book's way (stores and festivals refusing to stock the book, less fancy marketing for the book). Consider how nobody's gay that we know of in Twilight or the Hunger Games... consider Dumbledore being revealed as gay—but not, crucially, in the books themselves—in Harry Potter. Think about what a book being popular really *means*. (It doesn't

---

[1] Lili Saintcrow's *Betrayals*, sequel to her *Strange Angels*, is the other. You're welcome, curious reader!

mean the author gets to buy a golden helicopter.) It means that a lot of people read it—a lot of people get the message that, for instance, gay relationships shouldn't exist by reading books where they don't exist. I wish none of this were true, but it is; and since it is, I'm so happy that Cassandra Clare's books are in the world, and that they have been so wildly successful and beloved.

Cassandra Clare has achieved an enormous amount, because she's been able to send out this message to so many readers: Whoever you are, whatever you want—it's okay, and you are okay. You can be better than okay: You can be a hero.

We need more scandalous books by deviant wenches to tell us that.

Sarah Rees Brennan was born and raised in Ireland by the sea, where her teachers valiantly tried to make her fluent in Irish (she wants you to know it's not called Gaelic) but she chose to read books under her desk in class instead. She is the author of Team Human *and the Demon's Lexicon trilogy. Her new book is* Unspoken, *a romantic Gothic mystery about a girl who discovers her imaginary friend is a real boy.*

ABOUT THE EDITOR

#1 New York Times *bestselling author* **Cassandra Clare** *created the Mortal Instruments in 2004 with* City of Bones *(Simon & Schuster, 2007). Since then, the series has grown to five books, with a sixth due in 2014, and been joined by two spinoff trilogies and an upcoming film starring Jamie Campbell Power and Lily Collins. Clare's books have earned her numerous awards, including the American Library Association Teens Top Ten Title.*

REVISIT THE WORLD OF ENDER WIGGIN WITH
ORSON SCOTT CARD

EDITED BY

ORSON SCOTT CARD

ENDER'S WORLD

FRESH PERSPECTIVES ON THE SF CLASSIC
ENDER'S GAME

Edited by Orson Scott Card, *Ender's World* conscripts conscripts science fiction, fantasy, military, and young adult authors authors to offer new perspectives on the 1985 novel, from rethinking the child hero to the benefits (and perils) of using *Ender's Game* as a guide to life.

CONTRIBUTORS INCLUDE:

Hilari Bell
John Brown
Mette Ivie Harrison
Janis Ian
Aaron Johnston
Alethea Kontis

Mary Robinette
 Kowal
David Lubar and
 Allison S. Myers
Matt Nix
Col. Tom Ruby

Ken Scholes
Capt. John Schmitt
Neal Shusterman
Eric James Stone
Capt. John Schmitt